To John —
so many memories!

A SET OF
CURIOUS CHANCES

A Sequel to *Inclined to Dance and Sing*

from
Cynthia
with love

Cynthia Morey

June 2001

Prospero Books
46 West Street
Chichester
West Sussex
PO19 1RP

A CIP catalogue record for this book is available from the British Library.

ISBN 1 902320 25 5

Although every effort has been made to trace the present copyright holders, we apologise in advance for any unintentional omission or neglect and will be pleased to insert appropriate acknowledgment to companies or individuals in any subsequent edition of this publication.

Cover photo: Fleta (Marjorie Ward), Leila (CM) and Celia (Elizabeth Robson) in Sadler's Wells *Iolanthe*.

Back cover photo by Jonathan Dockar-Drysdale.

Printed and bound in Great Britain
Co-ordinated by Prospero Books

*To all my friends in the theatre,
with whom it has been such a joy to work.
And to all G & S addicts everywhere.*

Foreword

It is such a pleasure to me to be asked to write a foreword to Cynthia Morey's latest book *A Set of Curious Chances*. I found her first book *Inclined to Dance and Sing* an enchanting trip down my own memory lane and I simply could not put it down, so I cannot wait for the next instalment to begin.

The title of the new book is so apt because, although Cynthia and I have, sadly, never worked together, we have so much in common – by a set of curious chances! You see, although she had just left the D'Oyly Carte company as I joined, her reputation was still very much there, and so over the years I felt I really knew her and her work. I worked a great deal with the likes of John Reed, Don Adams, Gill Knight, Jenny Toye and John Fryatt later at the English National Opera, who all loved and admired Cynthia so much that when we finally met a few years ago at the Buxton Festival I had to remind them that I did not know her and needed some sort of introduction!

One other thing that unites us is that before I joined the Gilbert and Sullivan company, and in my holidays from the Royal College of Music, I also sang in pantomime with, yes, Cyril Fletcher and his wife! Curiouser and curiouser!

With my very best wishes for the success of this latest edition.

VALERIE MASTERSON C.B.E.

Prologue

Since the publication of my first literary attempt, *Inclined to Dance and Sing*, I have been both astonished and gratified to receive many requests for a sequel. 'Oh, I couldn't possibly –' was my first reaction, but the seed was sown.

I decided to take up the story from where I left off. I felt that tales of all the interesting people I have met in my many years in the theatre – in opera, musicals, plays and pantomime might make interesting reading, so *A Set of Curious Chances* (and some are curious indeed!) is an account of my post-D'Oyly Carte theatrical experiences. But fear not, Gilbert and Sullivan devotees – those two characters keep cropping up throughout. In fact, as you will find out, in recent years they seem to have taken over!

I have received much encouragement in my writing, and would like to thank all who have helped me and shown such interest, most particularly my husband, Anthony Jennings, for his unfailing patience and support. I was both delighted and honoured when Valerie Masterson agreed to write the foreword to this book. After her wonderful career in grand opera it is good to know that she still regards the Savoy operas with such affection. As we all do!

Cynthia Morey
Oxfordshire 2001

1.

'Goodbye! Good Luck! We'll come and see you!' Farewells and good wishes echoed and re-echoed down the corridors of the New Theatre, Oxford (Now the Apollo). It was May 13th 1957, and I had just sung my last *Patience* with the D'Oyly Carte Opera Company. For six years, straight from the Royal College of Music, I had been directed, protected, cosseted, guarded and guided by that venerable organisation, beginning as a chorister and ending up as a principal soprano. All this was about to change; I was on my own. That night I had I bid goodbye to Gilbert and Sullivan, and in a week's time I would dip my toe in the uncharted waters of commercial theatre. I regarded the chaos of my dressing room – not only was there all my make-up to be packed, but also an amazing collection of farewell cards and gifts (some of which I still have) from friends and colleagues. The blue and white striped dress I had worn for *Patience* that evening had been taken back to the wardrobe by the dresser; the blonde wig, striped stockings and black clod-hopping shoes (I should *not* miss those!) had also been collected – in fact, nothing remained to link me with my six years in the Carte. All that was in the past.

My first employer was Bridget D'Oyly Carte; my second was Cyril Fletcher. I can't imagine a greater contrast!

Cyril's wife, Betty Astell, who had always been his leading lady in their summer revue *Masquerade*, was, owing to ill health, unable to play her usual role in the 1957 season at Sandown on the Isle of Wight. That was where I came in. My new engagement followed on neatly; I had one free week before rehearsals for *Masquerade* began. During that week I went to the Fletchers' beautiful home in High Hurstwood, Sussex, to meet Betty, and to have costumes fitted for the show. She was a person of great charm, and made me very welcome, though it must have been rather sad to see her own costumes altered to fit someone else. She was very particular, making sure that everything was perfect, and supervising the whole process herself. I had wondered curiously what sort of dresses I would have to wear in a summer show, and had feared they might be rather tawdry and cheaply-made, in contrast to the high quality of those of the D'Oyly Carte; I needn't have worried. Everything was beautifully designed and well made. Betty and I were of a similar build – I was a little taller – so no great problems arose, and as I tried on the various costumes I began to feel an excited anticipation of the new and vastly different work I was about to undertake.

Preliminary rehearsals were to be at Dineley Studios in Marylebone Road. What a pleasant place that was – a large Georgian house, long since demolished to make way for much less attractive but more commercially viable property. It stood in lovely, if rather neglected gardens, and in one part of the grounds a large prefabricated building had been built, equipped with mirrors and barre for dance rehearsals. We, as a large company, were to use this.

On the first day I felt as nervous as on my introduction, six years previously, to the D'Oyly Carte Company. Many of the *Masquerade* cast had worked together before, and there were the usual effusive theatrical reunions. But there were also a number of newcomers, and we gravitated towards one another for moral support. I found that the company comprised six young girl dancers ('The Masquerade Lovelies' – what else?); Ian Francis – Cyril's 'feed' and supporting comic, who always seemed to wear a worried expression; Bruce Gordon – another 'funny' man; Anna Quayle – a rather eccentric comedienne; Betty Dayne and Frankie Murray, principal dancers; Gordon Holdom, baritone and vocal arranger; Scott Webber – a fine tenor; and all-rounders Robert Rose and Ken Baker. The latter doubled as stage manager and anything else that was required. Then of course there was the 'orchestra' – two pianos and percussion, presided over by Stanley Kilburn. Cyril was the hub around which everything revolved, and I – as well as doing my own solo spot (well placed in the second half of the show) had to 'feed' the comics, appear as all sorts of strange characters in sketches, and feature prominently in the spectacular scenes which were the highlight of each show. There were five programmes, changing on a Thursday, which meant that weekly visitors to Sandown could see two different performances during their stay.

I faced this new challenge with a certain amount of trepidation. I suppose I might have been regarded with awe by some members of the cast – I was, after all, an 'opera singer'! Had they but known it, the boot was most definitely on the other foot – I was rather more in awe of *them* – envying their experience in this slightly alarming new field. So many steps and moves to learn, so much unfamiliar music to memorise in a short time. Nina Walton, who had arranged the routines for several of Cyril's shows, was to choreograph *Masquerade*, and we spaced ourselves out on the dance floor to await her instructions. I must admit I was decidedly nervous – no D'Oyly Carte *pas bas* would be required here, I felt sure. I positioned myself strategically behind the dancers so that I could keep an eye on what they were doing – I had never even heard of 'step, ball, change' (a most rudimentary dance step) until that moment, and felt great embarrassment when it was assumed that everyone knew how to do it. However, a sideways glance at my more experienced colleagues showed me what it was (I realised I had been doing it for years in the Carte without knowing what it was called!) and I was soon dancing away with the rest. I've always been rather adept at covering up my inadequacies – after all, I've spent a lifetime at it!

One morning, when a scene in which I was not involved was being rehearsed, I sat at the far end of the room, taking the opportunity of learning some script. The sketch the others were working on was a skit on London Transport (ever topical). This is a refreshing change from Gilbert and Sullivan, I thought contentedly. Then from the other end of the room came a familiar sound which nearly made me fall off my chair. Anna Quayle was going through her part:

> 'One little lady bus conductress
> Leaping about like a gym instructress,
> Half civil servant, half seductress –
> Cooing in a voice so small:
> 'One more on top! That's all!!"

It wasn't the words, but the music which made me start – some of you will already have guessed what it was from the metre of the verse – yes, of course – the Three Little Maids trio from *The Mikado*. Here we are again, I sighed – just as I was thinking I'd got away from G & S!

After the London rehearsals, off we all went to the Isle of Wight, and the prospect of several months at the seaside stretched invitingly before us. I felt a great affection for the Island, having family links with it. My mother was born in Cowes, my grandfather was a shipping agent there, and my Uncle Louis had been the secretary of the Royal Yacht Squadron many years previously. Sandown Pavilion was a nicely-equipped little theatre at the end of the pier, and as I unpacked my make-up in the dressing room I was to share with Betty Dayne and Anna Quayle, I listened to the waves breaking below us. At the dress rehearsal I noticed Cyril regarding me with a quizzical expression. 'Is something wrong?' I asked. 'It's a pity you're not a blonde,' he said. I was horrified. 'Betty's a blonde, you know – all your costumes look so marvellous with fair hair,' he went on. Bleach my hair? The idea was preposterous. But the seed had been sown. The thought went round and round in my head, and I woke several times in the night, thinking about what Cyril had said.

The next morning found me at the best hairdresser in Sandown; I went in with brown hair and came out a blonde, part of me being quite horrified at what I had done. I rushed into a phone box and looked in the mirror (they still had mirrors in those vandal-free days) and burst into tears. 'Oh, oh –' I wailed, 'I was a principal soprano in an opera company, and now I'm a peroxide blonde on the end of the pier!' But when I went into rehearsal that afternoon the expression on Cyril's face made up for everything. The rest of the company crowded round, full of compliments – and there was no doubt that the costumes did look good with fair hair, especially under stage lighting. Oh, well, I thought,

I can always have it tinted back to its natural colour when I'm tired of it – which of course I eventually did.

The first night arrived, and the theatre was sold out. All sorts of civic dignitaries attended, and there were a number of actors and television personalities – friends of Cyril and Betty – among the audience. The show was warmly received, enthusiastically reviewed in the local press, and a successful season predicted. I began to relax and enjoy what I was doing and to understand the art involved in putting over a number, experimenting with movement and gesture. For the first time I was at liberty to interpret my songs as I wished, and develop my own personality.

I had taken a bedsit in Sandown, and I stayed put for a few weeks until I discovered that my every move was monitored by the most inquisitive landlady. Now, I do like my independence, and after much searching found a rather ramshackle chalet perched on the cliff overlooking the sea, which was much more to my liking, in spite of its rather primitive amenities. In retrospect, I am amazed that I dared to stay there on my own in that isolated position – I would not dream of doing so nowadays. But in 1957 I found the solitude delightful, and had no fears whatever of any intruder! I used to walk to the theatre every evening along the edge of the sea; it was usually about 6.30pm – all the holiday makers were in their hotels and guest houses for their evening meal, so the beach was quite deserted. I would do my 'warm-up' as I strolled along; it was most exhilarating, warbling away in that clear air.

Every performance began with the *Masquerade* opening chorus; the full company was on stage for this, immaculately dressed – the men in DJs and the girls in elegant gowns and long white gloves. There was a mad scramble to change after this, as the next item was invariably a series of quickfire gags and lightning sketches. I remember one of these was an operatic weather forecast, which I had to interrupt by making a wild dash across the stage in a swimsuit. I was hotly pursued by Frankie Murray, sporting an improbable white beard, while Cyril observed: 'the temperature's high in the eighties'!' I never lingered to see if this got a laugh, as another impossibly quick change followed. The show proceeded with various dance routines, sketches and comic spots, and the first half ended with a scene involving the whole company, one of which I remember was a potted music hall, with Cyril doing a marvellous George Robey. Anna Quayle was Marie Lloyd, and I Edna May.

Each programme included a spectacular scena – usually in the second half, and this featured everyone, with the exception of Cyril. I usually had some vocal number, or a duet with tenor or baritone. These items seem incredibly old fashioned today, but believe me, in 1957 they brought the house down! There was a Dutch scene, I remember, with all the girls in blue and white checked gingham and starched muslin caps; the set was liberally decked with windmills, and there was I, arm in arm with one of the men, doing an extraordinary clog dance and singing these immortal words:
> 'Strolling down by the Zuider Zee,
> Hans and me,
> Ve vill be,
> Ven ze vork of ze day is done –
> Oh, my – von't ve have fun!' etc etc.

The dancers followed this with a Dutch ballet, Betty and Frankie did a comedy routine, and finally we made our exit to great applause, skilfully avoiding a couple of outsize Delft plates on the way. Another programme found us in South America; I stood centre stage between two large cacti, wearing an exotic striped dress and an enormous wobbling sombrero, singing plaintively:

'Io te queros –
That's the song of the Cuban maid,
As she sings to her long lost lover
Such a passionate serenade'!

The dancers undulated gracefully around me; I endeavoured to sway as seductively as possible without losing my huge and precarious hat. That particular scena was not one of my favourites.

Another of these 'spectaculars', and one rather more to my liking was called 'Polka Promenade'. This was more akin to the sort of thing I was familiar with; the whole cast were elegantly dressed in Victorian style, and my own costume was a delight. I wore a gorgeous pale green crinoline, a matching bonnet lavishly trimmed with ostrich feathers, and carried a dainty parasol. I could go on for Mabel in this, I thought. But instead of 'Poor Wand'ring One' I sang 'In My Easter Bonnet' – not quite so classy, perhaps – but rather less demanding vocally!

Another 'extravaganza' was a beautifully set and lit underwater scene, dominated by an enormous oyster shell centre stage. This scene opened Part II of the show, so I had to conceal myself in this contraption at the end of the interval, before the curtain rose. On a given music cue I – as 'the Spirit of the Shell' had to raise the lid and arise gracefully, a huge and magnificent pearl in my hand. I was clad in a shimmering white sequin-covered gown, and holding the pearl aloft, proceeded to sing *The Song of India* from Rimsky Korsakov's *Sadko*, though I never quite understood what that particular aria had to do with the situation. As I finished the number, the dancers performed their underwater ballet, and on cue I tossed the pearl to Frankie Murray, who was appropriately clad in seaweedy leotard as the Sprite of the Sea. He caught it, lifted it on high, and continued the dance sequence with the girls. One night, however, I tossed it to him as usual, but he failed to catch it, and it went bounce, bounce, bounce across the stage – our priceless pearl was, after all, only a rubber ball painted silver. The magic of the scene was completely destroyed, and this event reduced us – and the audience – to helpless mirth. I longed to retreat into my oyster shell and pull down the lid, but dared not – I had to stand there in dignified agony until the lights began to fade at the end of the scene, and only then could I escape.

Probably the most effective scena – visually – was 'The Story of Dresden China'; the curtain arose on a really charming scene, with the whole company dressed as delicate eighteenth century china figures, in white satin costumes and powdered wigs. We were 'frozen' in attitudes representing Dresden figurines; the 'potter' stood at one side of the stage telling the story, and one by one, as the music began, we came to life and performed a series of minuets and gavottes, interspersed with appropriate vocal numbers. Finally the music and lights slowly faded, and we froze again into our original poses. However quaint all that may sound nowadays, believe me – the jolly holiday audiences in 1957 Sandown just loved it!

Cyril's comedy spot occurred, predictably, towards the end of the second half. It was quite long, very funny, and the audience enjoyed every minute of it. He usually included a couple of the 'odd odes' for which he was so well known. We must remember that Cyril Fletcher was at that time one of the big names in comedy, and a considerable draw. Of course, summer shows in the *Masquerade* format do not exist today, and even if they did, they would have to feature a pop star or a soap idol to attract any size of audience – not to mention the daunting level of amplification which would be demanded. Coming from a 'mike-less' generation, when the art of voice projection was taken for granted, the present day decibel level fills me with despair. Way back in the fifties the name of Cyril Fletcher plus dancers and good supporting cast was sufficiently attractive to draw capacity houses.

My own solo spot immediately preceded Cyril's, and he set and lit my numbers most attractively. I had to provide my own dresses for this, and he always studied the colour I was wearing when lighting, also the mood of the numbers I had selected to sing. I had chosen a mix of the lighter operatic arias, such as the *Laughing Song* from *Die Fledermaus*, or 'pop' arias – *O My Beloved Father* from Puccini's *Gianni Schicchi* was a great favourite. I also included medleys from modern musicals – *Carousel, Oklahoma* and *Salad Days*, which was then in its heyday at the Vaudeville Theatre. (No Gilbert and Sullivan, devotees will observe!)

Once we had presented all five shows life became a little easier. There was usually a brief rehearsal before each change of programme, and the dancers, under the watchful eye of Betty Dayne, worked for a short while every day, but otherwise we had more time to ourselves and were able to enjoy the amenities of Sandown. We did have a number of 'official' engagements; judging beauty competitions and bonny baby contests, attending fetes, selling flags, but the duties were not too onerous on the whole. Cyril was a wonderful boss and made sure he ran a happy company. But he could be – occasionally – a little unorthodox. It was not at all unusual while doing your shopping in the town on a Friday morning, to find a car drawing up alongside you, and Cyril leaning out. 'I think it's all here,' he would say as he handed you a bundle of notes, 'better count it!' And off he drove – I have never received my salary like that before – or since!

That was a very happy season and we all got along extremely well. I enjoyed the novelty of the work I was doing, and found it easier and more rewarding as I settled into the routine and began to find my feet. I learned a great deal from Betty Dayne, who had done many shows with Cyril, and found her an invaluable help with movement and staging. I was intrigued with Anna Quayle – one of life's eccentrics. Sadly, she was not really at ease in *Masquerade*; she had a wonderful, zany sense of humour which I fear went over the heads of the jolly holiday crowds. I loved her act, but the response from the audience to her way-out character studies and sophisticated sketches must have been disappointing for her. As I anticipated, she went on to great success – *Stop the World – I Want to Get Off* with Anthony Newley in 1961 brought her to the notice of West End theatregoers. Her sense of humour was just too eccentric for a seaside summer show.

Old colleagues from the D'Oyly Carte did keep their promise to visit – John Reed in particular. I think he was intrigued – and maybe just a touch envious – to see me doing something so entirely different from Gilbert and Sullivan. John is talented in so many ways that there is no doubt at all that he could have stepped up on to the stage of the Pavilion then and there and joined the show. But as we have seen in later years, it's just as well that he did not, or the D'Oyly Carte would have lost one of its brightest stars. What's more, when the season in Sandown came to an end, I was out of work and John wasn't!

2.

September arrived, and Sandown began to take on a rather sad 'end of season' look. I stood at the pier entrance one evening before the show and watched idly as the wind, which now held a definite touch of autumn, caught up some scraps of paper and blew them along the deserted promenade. The nights were imperceptibly drawing in, and the holiday crowds – and consequently the audiences – were beginning to thin out. Eventually we found ourselves in the last week of the run, and in a way we were not really sorry. One thing loomed large on the horizon, however – unemployment – a spectre I had not had to face before. What was the next step to take, I wondered – everyone else seemed to find work through an agent, and I had not so far had to go along that road. There was no time to lose – I would 'do the rounds' as soon as I was back in London.

That night Cyril waylaid me in the corridor. 'How would you like to come and do pantomime for us?' he asked. 'Oh, I *would*,' I replied – 'very much.' We're at the New Theatre, Northampton this year,' he said. 'It's *The Sleeping Beauty* that's you, of course. Good – we'll see about the contract.' And off he whirled to make his entrance. I was delighted. Rehearsals would not begin until the beginning of December – that left an awkward gap, with October and November unaccounted for. Oh well, I thought – I'll be able to fill in with a short engagement (ah – the optimism of inexperience!). But at least I had something on the horizon to look forward to.

The last night at the Pavilion attracted a packed house. Lots of hoteliers and guest house proprietors turned up, and local people with whom we'd made friends during our stay. *Masquerade* went with a real sparkle, and there were the usual emotional farewells after the final curtain, with promises to keep in touch. Several of the cast I would meet again for pantomime, and that was something to look forward to. I packed all the dresses I had worn for my solo spot in a large trunk, which I sent on ahead – you could do this for five shillings in those days! A few days later I was in London, and the somewhat dispiriting search for an agent began.

I looked in *The Stage*, I asked friends, and finally I did find an agent. I climbed some rickety stairs in a tall narrow building just off Piccadilly Circus to discover, tucked away in a tiny office like a spider in a web, Mildred Challenger, who ran the Encore Agency. The small room was overflowing with photographs, posters and bulging files. Mildred peered at me doubtfully. She showed no enthusiasm whatever on hearing I had been a principal in the D'Oyly Carte, and seemed to consider it no recommendation at all for finding work in the commercial theatre. She brightened up somewhat when I told her of my season with Cyril Fletcher, and she did find me an engagement – one week in Variety at the Continental Palace, Hull. I did not enjoy this at all.

The theatre was a newly-refurbished venue; the audience sat round at tables and were served with drinks during the show. I suppose a sophisticated nightclub ambience had been the intention, for most acts performed both on stage and among the patrons, descending a purpose-built set of steps to do so. I had to sing two numbers in my allotted spot, then participate in the Irish finale, in which everyone was involved. Since I was billed – once again – as 'The Star from the D'Oyley Carte Opera Company' (why do they always spell it like that – we are not a set of lace mats), I decided to sing my old favourite 'The Laughing Song' from *Die Fledermaus* and follow it up with a popular Italian number of that time, 'Volare'. I arrived at the appointed rehearsal hour on the Monday morning for the band call to find most of the other acts already there, waiting around on the bleak empty stage. Although my work with Cyril Fletcher had been so very different from that of the D'Oyly Carte, I had nevertheless still been part of a company, with a similar feeling of comradeship. Now I was absolutely alone.

I noticed that the other participants had laid their band parts down along the front of the stage. I made a move to do the same, but was stopped in my tracks by an irate little man who turned out to be Reg 'Taking the Mike' Lloyd (Comedian)! 'You can't put your music *there!*' he said crossly, 'you're jumping the queue – put it over *there!*' and he indicated the far end of the row. I hastily did as he said, having no wish to start out on the wrong foot. Thus I learned my first lesson in the Variety world; apparently band calls were a case of 'first come, first served', not order of programme, and places were booked by the position of your music in the queue. That explained why everyone showed up so early. When my turn eventually came, after a succession of comics, other singers and Jack Whiteley's Eight Zio Angels ('Dancing to Delight') I handed my music to the MD, who regarded it with deep suspicion. He held my copy of 'The Laughing Song' by one corner, as if it was something faintly offensive – I believe this was his first encounter with Johann Strauss. We got through it without mishap – it is a fairly straightforward piece – or so it had to be at the Continental Palace, Hull, where I wisely refrained from any subtleties. Next was 'Volare', which had been a great hit in the UK for the past few weeks, though I had discovered it before that while on holiday in Italy, whence it came. The MD took the copy and sighed, 'Oh – not *this* again! We've had it every week for the last couple of months!' This pronouncement, needless to say, filled me with confidence. We went through it, and I discovered that I had to take a trailer mike and go down into the audience during the number, which prospect did not imbue me with joyous anticipation.

In the evening I was filled with grim determination. I put on my most flamboyant dress – a strapless, flame-coloured, full-skirted affair, which I hoped would not trip me up as I descended the steps. After putting on an exotic make-up topped by an extravagant hair-do, which I achieved by much back-combing and lacquer, I looked at myself in the mirror and burst out laughing. The funny side of the situation dawned on me, and I quite enjoyed myself in the end. I don't know if the patrons of the Continental Palace appreciated the unusual opportunity of hearing an aria from *Die Fledermaus*, but they applauded dutifully. *Volare* was much more to their taste, and I descended from the stage, mike in hand, to mingle with the audience. A portly gent at the front with a pint of beer in one hand leered at me and beckoned invitingly, so I obligingly sat on his knee for a moment, to the delight of the patrons, then, blowing him a kiss, I left him and returned to the stage, where I gave the number a big finish. The applause was quite generous as I took my bow, but I was not sorry that my first Variety act was over. Only five more to go, I told myself as I made my way to the dressing room. There was just the Irish finale remaining that evening, during which I had to give an appealing rendering of 'Shure, a little bit of heaven fell from out the sky one day' and join in the chorus of 'If you're Irish, come into the parlour' – not too demanding. I decided to change into an emerald green dress for this piece of theatrical magic.

Somehow the week passed and I found myself packing up on the Saturday night with considerable relief. I had more than a month to get through before pantomime rehearsals commenced, and some sort of job must be found. Going on the dole, which most theatricals did between jobs was all very well, but the business of 'signing on' and the constant pressure to take regular employment could be very tedious. Soon after my return to London I chanced to bump in to Lorna Pobjoy, an old D'Oyly Carte colleague, in Oxford Street. We retired to the nearest coffee shop to catch up on all the news and commiserate with each other on the current work situation. Lorna confessed to me that she was doing a temporary job as an usherette at the Academy Cinema. 'There are a lot of pro's there,' she said, 'and they're always coming and going – why not see if there's a vacancy?' I pondered on the idea. 'I don't much fancy it,' I replied doubtfully, 'still – there are several weeks before I start rehearsing...perhaps I'll enquire.' I found out that there was indeed an evening job, so I decided to take it – it wouldn't be for long, after all. What a comical situation! Lorna worked the afternoon shift, and I went in as she was going out. She took off her uniform, I put it on, she handed me her torch, and away I went! That was in the days of continuous performances, when usherettes had to show patrons to their seats in the dark, and shine a torch along the row. What a boring job that was – I almost wished I was back in Hull – but not quite! One thing must be said in the Academy's favour, however – it was a venue for avant garde, arty films, and attracted quite a superior clientele. I even got a ten shilling tip one evening from a very nice man – that was a lot in those days. How funny, I thought – he might have seen me as Yum-Yum a few months ago – a good thing it's dark!

The film showing during my stint at the cinema was Ingmar Bergman's *Wild Strawberries*, in Swedish, of course, and I have to confess that although I saw it countless times, I never found out what it was all about. Still, I did pick up a few words of Swedish during my stay. But, oh, what a relief when the time came to begin *Sleeping Beauty* rehearsals, and I could hand in my uniform and my torch for ever!

The pantomime company met at dear old Dineley Studios, now familiar to me, and this time it was my turn to greet old friends. Cyril Fletcher, of course, was Dame – Queen of Happykin Land, with Ian Francis, who had been his 'feed' in Sandown, as the King – and a very henpecked one at that. I was very fortunate to have John Boulter, of Black and White Minstrel fame as my Prince Florizel. We had some charming duets, written by Betty Astell herself, and it was a great pleasure to have such an excellent tenor to work with. I made some good friends during that season in Northampton, and we had a lot of laughs. Cyril had gathered together his usual happy company, and it paid off in performance. One of the cast, Patrick O'Connell, who played

'Liquorice' – a tiny part as a servant, later made quite a name for himself in television. Anyone who remembers *The Brothers* – a series featuring a family-run haulage firm – may recall him as Edward, the eldest brother, and he has many other TV plays to his credit.

Pantomime is hard work – there's no denying the fact. Over the Christmas and New Year period we were doing thirteen shows a week – twice nightly, plus a matinee on Saturdays. It was quite daunting to hear the stage manager in the wings saying 'Quarter of an hour, please' as you were taking your curtain call for the previous performance. As soon as the house tabs came in there was a mad rush to the dressing room to scramble back into your opening costume. A quick repair of your make-up, a lightning cup of tea – if you were lucky – then it was 'overture and beginners' and off we went again. The three shows on Saturday were a marathon; the middle one at five o'clock was the worst. The two o'clock was fine, because you were feeling fresh and full of energy; the eight o'clock was all right because you knew it was the last, but oh – the one in between! I did a song sheet number with Cyril in the second act, with audience participation, and urging them on with great enthusiasm to join in 'Who put the dots on the dalmatian dog?' three times in one day was no mean feat.

Costumes were, as in *Masquerade*, of a very high standard. My 'walk down' dress was stunning – an enormous crinoline of silver-green brocade with a long train. One of the conditions Cyril insisted on when drawing up my contract was that I should remain a blonde for the duration of the pantomime. A long matching fall of ringlets was ordered for me from Wig Creations, and imparted a fairytale effect. It apparently looked very effective spread out on the pillow in the sleeping scene when I lay on my couch awaiting the Prince's waking kiss – a favourite moment in the show.

The Sleeping Beauty was certainly a family affair. Although Betty Astell was not performing in it this time, she had written the piece, composed most of the music and designed the costumes. Cyril undertook the direction and lighting – he was particularly good at the latter – and we were a very close company; this was a wonderful antidote to my lonely experience in Hull. As in Sandown there were civic functions to attend, parties, receptions and press interviews, so with our busy performance schedule there was very little free time. But I dreaded the end of the run, with the prospect of unemployment.

I am tempted to gloss over the next year of my foray into the commercial side of the business, but because I am trying to stick to facts and because some of my adventures have had their hilarious moments, I have decided to leave nothing out. Also, it was the last really bad patch before things began to look up – though I didn't know that at the time. At the end of February I was again looking for work, calling frequently on Mildred Challenger and reading *The Stage* from cover to cover. One day I noticed an advertisement for demonstrators to work at the Ideal Home Exhibition; now, this would be a good temporary fill-in, I thought, as it only ran for four weeks – surely something would turn up after that? I telephoned, obtained an interview, and went to see the advertiser at his office in North London. I found that I would be required to man a stand at Olympia with several other girls, where we would demonstrate and extol the virtues of floral-scented disinfectant sprays. This seemed rather a fragrant occupation, and as the engagement was for a limited time, the salary and commission good, and the boss a kindly man, I decided to take it on.

My workmates turned out to be most congenial – two were out-of-work pro's like me, and between us we organised our shifts to suit ourselves, which took care of the odd audition. I think the boss was amazed and delighted by the amount of stock we shifted; his idea of recruiting staff from the theatrical community had paid off. Commission soared to gratifying levels as we turned our charm on the mesmerised public, few of whom escaped without parting with some cash. I quite enjoyed myself at Olympia, getting to know the folk on the other stands and sampling their wares. As we neared the end of our four-week contract, the boss approached me confidentially. 'Would you consider a permanent job with us?' he asked. 'I'd like you to travel round the country demonstrating our products in large stores, but first you would supervise our stand at the Scottish Ideal Home Exhibition, and train the other demonstrators.' I tried to explain that I had only required some temporary work between theatre engagements, but he wouldn't take no for an answer, and before I realised what was happening, I was on my way to Edinburgh. The exhibition was, as in London, highly successful. Someone, however, found out about my past, and the press turned up. This could be useful, I thought, as they took photographs. A glance at the paper next day dispelled any hopes in that direction. A large picture of me, holding aloft one of the dreaded disinfectant sprays graced the centre page. Underneath was the caption: 'The Star and the Squirt'.

I worked for this firm for a few more weeks, frantically seeking a job in the theatre meanwhile. At last Mildred belatedly found me a summer season, and I bid farewell to my kind boss. 'Any time you'd like to work for us...' he said pleadingly as I edged towards the door of his office. I thanked him and fled.

The summer show I had taken on so desperately was at the Little Theatre, Tenby – long since vanished, I expect. Tenby is a delightful spot, but oh – what a ghastly show! It was only a six-hander, and a more bizarre assortment of artists it would be impossible to imagine. The manager – white-haired and in his late sixties I imagine, was a sort of compère, and his 'girl friend' – not far behind him in years, and ahead of him in weight – the sour-faced leading lady. She was billed as 'The Vital Spark', which decription left me speechless. The musical interest was provided by an accordionist, who was having a problem with one of his hands. His act would more effectively have been billed as 'Guess the Tune', for many of the notes he played were not at all those he intended, and the result was somewhat unusual. To add variety to the programme we had a magician whose every other trick went (unintentionally) wrong, leaving the audience perplexed. Next came a veteran all-rounder who gave us assorted vocal gems accompanied by some peculiar soft shoe dancing. He wore the most extraordinary wig, which he made no effort to disguise – goodness knows how old he was – in his spirited rendering of 'Mother Kelly's Doorstep' he looked as if he pre-dated the old song by a fair number of years. Then of course there was the comedian – words fail me at this point – I shall say no more. I was relieved to find that there was an extremely good accompanist; she was a local lady, properly trained – she probably received half-a-crown per show for her efforts.

Of course, I had my solo spot, providing my own dresses – the ones I had worn for *Masquerade* were more than adequate. To say I brought the house down with my singing sounds rather conceited, but in view of the competition I had, any other outcome would have indicated that I should give up the business at once. (Some of the audience reaction might of course have been caused by sheer relief!) One item in the programme will remain for ever in my memory. I used to enter to the music of McDowall's 'To a Wild Rose', and stand at the side of the stage, singing 'Slender flower, tender flower, gossamer and airy', whereupon the Vital Spark would bourré on heavily in a pink net tutu and proceed to execute a leaden routine. When I got to the words 'fashioned by a fairy' it was as much as I could do to finish the number with a straight face.

In spite of the dreadful show, I did enjoy my summer in Tenby very much. I found the most wonderful digs in a small cottage with a lady aptly named Mrs Smiles. She helped me to augment my meagre income by arranging for me to sing a solo every Sunday at evensong in the church, for which I received the welcome sum of one guinea. I found another way to earn some extra cash, thanks to my early art school training. One day I took my painting equipment and discovered a quiet spot overlooking Tenby harbour. I set out to do a pen and wash drawing of the attractive scene, and was rather pleased with the way it turned out. There was a souvenir shop just across the way, and when I called in to buy some postcards I showed my picture to the proprietor. He was quite taken with it, and thought visitors to Tenby might be interested in buying that sort of thing, with the result that I sold a fair number of sketches during my ten week stay. I certainly didn't make a fortune, but any addition to my minute salary was a help. I was almost sorry to leave at the end of the season, and to say goodbye to Mrs Smiles, with whom I corresponded for many years.

Back in London I managed to coast along with one or two Masonic dinners and a few concerts for a while, hoping to keep going until pantomime rehearsals commenced. Mildred had secured me a contract to play principal boy in *Dick Whittington* at the Palace Theatre, Westcliff for the 1958 season, and I was looking forward to this, realising that playing boy would be a new and challenging experience. It seemed that each successive engagement taught me something to add to my growing experience in the theatre, though I don't think I learned anything at all from my stint in Tenby – unless it was the art of keeping a straight face against tremendous odds.

I did a few Masonic dinners with a baritone who had noticed me when I sang in an introductory concert on joining the Concert Artists' Association. Apparently he took a fancy to me, as he offered me a string of dates for forthcoming Masonics. This is great, I thought, until after the third dinner I discovered that he expected to continue our duets after the concert, and in more intimate surroundings. This notion did not appeal to me at all – in any case, I did not find him

in the least attractive, and after I told him I'd rather be on
the dole, our association ended abruptly. A temporary post
as a waitress followed, in a small coffee shop called The
Mustard Pot, tucked away in Kingly Street, a stone's throw
from Piccadilly Circus. I found this infinitely preferable to
continuing my partnership with the amorous baritone. The
Mustard Pot was a congenial place to work – only light snacks
were served, and the other waitress was a most superior type
– what was she doing there? I asked myself – (or *I*, for that
matter?!) Her only drawback was that she rushed to serve
everyone who came in before I had a chance to do so, thereby
pocketing all the tips. However, when the lunchtime rush
was on, we both worked at full stretch, which evened things
out a bit.

One day there was a drama: the cook failed to turn up, and
the boss – a nice little lady – was close to tears. 'Don't worry,'
I said rashly, 'I'll take over for now.' I didn't realise what I
was saying. All was well during the morning – coffee and
danish pastries were no problem – but as the café filled up
for lunch, chaos reigned in my tiny kitchen. I was buttering
toast, scrambling eggs, grilling bacon, stirring soup – all at
the same time, as orders piled up relentlessly. Somehow I
coped, and apart from one or two plates returned because
the toast was a bit burnt round the edges, nothing serious
occurred. I was shattered at the end of the session, but the
boss was full of gratitude – I believe she gave me an extra
ten shillings! Just as I heaved a sigh of relief I learned that
the cook would be away till the following Monday, and could
I possibly continue in the kitchen for the rest of the week?
My heart sank, but somehow I managed – luckily it was my
last week, for rehearsals for *Dick Whittington* were about to

start. On the Friday the boss took me aside. 'Would you consider a permanent post as manageress?' she asked. I had a job not to burst out laughing. It seemed that every time I took a temporary job I was offered promotion! If only this would happen in the theatre, I thought.

On arriving in Westcliff I was delighted to find my old friend Frankie Murray from *Masquerade* was to play Idle Jack, so plenty of hilarity, both on and off stage would be ensured. It felt really good to be part of a company once more. The technique of playing principal boy was something on which I had to concentrate, remembering always to stand correctly, deliver my lines in quite a different way from usual, and stride about the stage in an appropriately boyish manner. This was all new to me; I had of course done many things since the dainty poses of Phyllis or the tiny shuffling steps of Yum-Yum, but so far I had always been feminine. Now it was entirely different.

Dick Whittington was a good, traditional production, with dear, homely Jerry Jerome as Sarah the Cook, and a competent supporting cast. Diana Chadwick was Alice Fitzwarren – I was destined to meet her again later on in my career – but more of that anon. The show was not perhaps quite of the standard of Cyril Fletcher's pantomimes, (I noticed that the programmes were only 3d, whereas Cyril's had been 4d! – perhaps that indicated something!) but it was nicely staged and efficiently directed. There was, inevitably, the obligatory songsheet, only this time it was 'Why does a red cow give white milk when it only eats green grass' instead of 'Who put the dots on a dalmatian dog' – both poetic gems. One of the most touching moments must surely have been when I knelt at the footlights, my arm round my cat Tommy, and sang (with an affecting break in my voice) 'I'll get by – as long as I have you'! Not a dry eye in the house.

The whole thing was great fun, of course – pantomime always is – but as the season wore on I began to think seriously about my professional future. Summer shows (reputable ones, that is!) and pantomimes were all very well, but what of the intervening time? Odd concerts – weekly dates – these did not amount to much over the year. Since leaving the D'Oyly Carte I had learned two very important things: I'd had enough of this hand-to-mouth existence, and I preferred working as a member of a company.

Everything seemed to point to Sadler's Wells.

3.

Once I had made up my mind what direction my future career should take – if fate would permit – I lost no time in seeking an audition at Sadler's Wells. This was a simple matter, for as it turned out I had applied at a most fortuitous moment. The Carl Rosa Company closed in the summer of 1958; most of the chorus and orchestra and many of the principal singers went into the hastily-formed Touring Opera 58, and subsequently out on an autumn tour. Important events were to take place on their return. Sadler's Wells were to launch a second company with the intention of providing opera in London and the regions at the same time. The management were able to expand in this way as a result of the enormous success of *The Merry Widow* at the Coliseum, starring June Bronhill and Thomas Round. The old Carl Rosa formed the backbone of this new 'T' Company, as it was called, but extra choristers were needed, and recruitment was about to begin when I applied for an audition.

Selecting a suitable audition piece reminded me of the time, more than eight years previously, when I had to choose a song for the D'Oyly Carte. But this time it would not be a 'bright English song' (as requested by the Carte) but an operatic aria. I've always maintained that it's wise to produce an obscure piece for audition purposes. The panel of adjudicators will very likely have sat through ten Mimis and fourteen Cio Cio Sans, and maybe a sprinkling of Susannas – something out of the ordinary may shake them out of their lethargy and make them sit up and listen. Also – and this is an important point – they will be familiar with all the pitfalls of the well-known aria, and will be watching out for the candidate to fall into them. With a more way-out piece it is possible to get away with quite a lot – a process at which I have always been fairly adept.

With these things in mind I decided on 'Gathering Berries', Snegourotchka's aria from Rimsky-Korsakov's *The Snow Maiden*. Fortunately it had to be sung in English – had the original Russian been required, I should certainly have had second thoughts. It is a very attractive song, and there is an impressive top B natural at the end, which sounds suitably spectacular, but which in fact is quite easy to bring off successfully. I arrived at the Wells in good time, and was directed to the circle bar, where a few other candidates were waiting. When my turn came I was escorted down to the stage, introduced, and after a few words with the accompanist I sang my aria. I was duly thanked by the panel, asked some questions about my past musical experience, and told I would hear from them in a few days. Then it was back home to wait in suspense for my letter of acceptance or rejection. In retrospect I would assume that the audition panel had included Norman Tucker, Tom Hammond, and possibly John Barker, who was Chorus Master of 'T' Company at that time.

I honestly do not know what my next step would have been if I had failed my audition for the Wells, and while awaiting my letter from them, I pondered long on what other avenues might be available to me. I hardly dared to open the letter when it came – but I needn't have worried – I was successful. So it was back to the chorus, to start all over again. It had taken me three and a half years in the D'Oyly Carte to rise to principal status; would it ever be possible for me to become a soloist in grand opera? After all, I was still very much a light lyric soprano, and dramatic roles would always be out of my reach. But such thoughts at this stage were counter-productive. I had obtained what I had set out to achieve: a regular job in a large and prestigious company; this had been my main objective. In later years many D'Oyly Carte singers made this transition to the Wells – some had been principals like myself – Jennifer Toye, for instance, who had sung many of the soprano roles; Neville Griffiths, Joseph Riordan and John Fryatt – three notable tenors who, after playing leading parts, happily settled down in the Sadler's Wells (later English National Opera) chorus – some for many years.

When I arrived at the stage door on the first day of rehearsal, memories came flooding back, and I felt a momentary twinge of sadness. Sadler's Wells was no new territory to me. I had spent six weeks there with the Carte in the summer of 1953, consequently I knew my way around backstage, and was fairly familiar with the warren of corridors, steps and dressing rooms. Yet this time everything felt different. Before, I had been a member of a visiting company; now this was *my* theatre, *my* dressing room. That first day marked the beginning of my love affair with the Wells – a love affair that was to last for many years. I still feel a distinct sense of loss when I realise that the old theatre no longer exists. I know it had its drawbacks; the wing space was inadequate for dance, the foyer cramped and inconvenient, the facilities outdated – but I loved it just the same. The dressing rooms were basic, but spacious, the chorus rooms large, and divided into separate bays; there was plenty of room for costumes, and the windows actually opened, letting in fresh air, albeit with a fair proportion of carbon monoxide from Rosebery Avenue below. I have fond memories of sunbathing on that grimy roof during rehearsals, and frantically throwing on some clothes when our call came to go on stage.

On that first day I made my way up endless flights of stone steps to the opera rehearsal room on the top floor, the rickety lift being, as usual, full to bursting point. The room was very large and light; rows of chairs were set out in readiness, many already filled with chattering choristers. I made sure which side the sopranos sat, then selected a vacant chair in the second row. I gazed round with curiosity at my new colleagues. How did they compare with the D'Oyly Carte chorus? They seemed fairly similar, I decided. There were the same stocky, rather short tenors (forgive me, any tall slim tenor who may be reading this!), the somewhat larger baritones, altos of various shapes and sizes, including several of the more Junoesque variety, and the usual assortment of sopranos. But there was a subtle difference. It seemed to me that when the Carte auditioned prospective choristers, they were looking for types as well as vocal quality. More often than not, their principals were promoted from the chorus – understudies, too – and I imagine the management always had this in mind. Also, I suppose they had to be aware that the girls would be appearing as fairies, schoolgirls, bridesmaids, etc., so the larger ladies might be more difficult to accommodate! Having said this, I seem to remember there were one or two buxom altos lurking towards the back of the stage during my time in the Carte, for after all, understudies for the principal contralto roles must be accommodated. But in a company presenting grand opera, all physiques – within reason – are acceptable. The voice is paramount, and the peasants, courtiers, townsfolk etc. that choristers are normally expected to play can be of any shape and size – indeed, the more characterful the individual, the better. We all sat waiting for John Barker, the chorus master, to appear. The seat beside me was still empty, so I supposed there was one more soprano to come. Then the door opened, and a vision appeared in the shape of a very attractive girl with long red hair and nails to match. She wore a short, tight skirt, and shoes with the highest stiletto heels I have ever seen. There were some whistles from the men – (that was the era when such a reaction was regarded as a compliment; I myself am still inclined to regard it as such, though I regret to say I find the occurrence becoming increasingly rare these days!) The new arrival was not in the least disconcerted – she flashed a dazzling smile in the direction of the men, then seeing the vacant chair next to mine, came and sat beside me. 'I'm Suzanne Steele,' she said. 'Are you new, too?' I replied that I was, and introduced myself, but further conversation was cut short by the arrival of John Barker, with a pile of vocal scores. He was a dark-haired, rather shy-looking man, with a slight impediment in his speech, and very efficient at his job, if a little pedantic. Discipline during his rehearsals was generally good, though just occasionally things could get a bit rowdy. John had endless patience, repeatedly thumping out vocal lines on the piano for various sections of the chorus, during which time those of us not concerned would start to chat, causing him to become annoyed and call us to order.

Scores were given out, and we started our first rehearsal with *Carmen*. All the old hands had performed this popular opera countless times, and sang lustily; this was a great help to us new ones, and of course the score is so full of well-known melodies that it was a fairly easy piece to begin with, especially for the sopranos, who usually have the tune. I was impressed with the volume and quality of the singing; the size of the chorus was much larger than that of the D'Oyly Carte, so the body of sound was obviously greater. During the fifties the numbers in the Carte chorus had dwindled to around thirty-two; I have often looked at photographs of old productions and marvelled at the stage crowded with choristers – they must have produced a much louder sound than that to which we had become accustomed. For instance, in my time we never had 'twenty lovesick maidens' in *Patience*, or the 'two dozen we' mentioned in *The Gondoliers* – we just hoped the audience wouldn't count us!

The mid-morning break came, and there was a general stampede for coffee in the canteen, which in those days was at the rear of the stalls. I was not so efficient then at being first in the queue – that was an art I perfected later. This establishment was run by Florrie and Elsie – two rather masculine-looking ladies in navy suits and white blouses; they were delightful, always smiling, but ever ready with a bit of acid repartee if the occasion so demanded. While we waited to be served, I chatted to Suzanne and discovered she had recently been in *Kismet* at the Stoll, a fine theatre sadly demolished not long afterwards. I detected that under her smiling exterior lay a steadfast determination to to make headway in opera, and not to remain in the chorus a moment longer than she could help. I wished I could feel as confident of success. I soon found out that Suzanne had a wicked sense of humour, and as it turned out, we became great friends.

That rehearsal was the first of many, with costume fittings slotted into the schedule. This was easy for the girls, as many of the new ones were made on the premises; others were brought from the store for us, to be fitted in the wardrobe. I grew to have great respect for the Sadler's Wells wardrobe; it was an extremely efficient organisation, and excellent costumes were created with the minimum extravagance, and none of the waste which seems to go on in larger opera houses these days. Wigs, too, were often brought from stock, re-dressed, re-styled, tinted or dyed as required, and constantly re-used. Perhaps some of the chorus costumes were not made from the exceptionally high quality materials used by the D'Oyly Carte, but we must remember that they only had to last for a fraction of the time. Operas came in and out of the repertoire – some were revivals, others new productions, but none – unlike the Carte – were toured incessantly, year after year. When operetta came to Sadler's Wells it was another story. It was always beautifully dressed, and in costumes of the highest quality, for it was performed nightly, sometimes for a season, and constantly re-introduced into the repertoire.

The D'Oyly Carte repertoire was obviously set within rigid limits, although this had not always been the case; when the company was first formed, many non-Gilbert and Sullivan pieces had been performed. But in later years it was restricted solely to the G & S operas, which was really rather a pity. After a few years as a chorister with the company, it was difficult not to go into the dressing room at night and sigh, 'Oh – it's *The Mikado* again!' knowing that once more you would go through the same routines, in the same costumes, at the same tempi – for nothing would ever change. Having said this, after I left things did change – a little – though even when an opera was newly set and dressed, it seemed to me that it was very much the mixture as before. Not so at Sadler's Wells. You might do half a dozen *Bohèmes* in one season, then it would disappear for an unspecified period, to return afresh, probably with a different conductor, change of cast, and maybe in a new guise.

The constant variety of work appealed to me greatly. Fresh operas, with new conductors and producers (incidentally, the term 'director', which comes to us from the USA did not – and still does not – apply to opera) kept us permanently on our toes, and made for a stimulating life in the chorus. There were often small parts to be allotted, too, and these – although given for suitability and merit, were pretty fairly distributed among the choristers. Ever-changing work conditions like these probably accounted for the fact that a large proportion of singers stayed with the company for many years.

Back in the chorus I might be – but I felt sure I was going to enjoy life at Sadler's Wells.

4.

Touring with the Wells was a little like touring with the D'Oyly Carte, though conditions had obviously improved since the early fifties. I nearly always shared digs with Suzanne, who had acquired a Ford Zephyr. This made all the difference in the world – in any case, I can't imagine how she could possibly have coped with travelling by train. She would throw all her things into the car in the most haphazard fashion, and was always accompanied by an enormous bag of multi-coloured stiletto-heeled shoes – at least twenty pairs, at a rough guess. We stayed in many of my old digs and were welcomed warmly; it was good to see old friends again – for that is what many of those wonderful landladies had now become. Gone was the official train call for those people who still travelled by rail, which at that time was the majority of the company. Now everyone was given their fare and trusted to report at the right time and place on the Monday. Life was much less regimented than I remembered from my old days of touring, but then, life had changed – even in the D'Oyly Carte, I supposed...

When playing theatres in the north, we made hair-raising journeys at break-neck speed down the M1 (then very new) early on Sunday morning, and equally terrifying ones back on the Monday. I wasn't awfully keen on the dizzy speed at which Sue drove, but she was a very good driver, so I just sat back and hoped for the best – and that was before the days of seatbelts! One of these trips comes clearly to mind – I think it was from Leeds, where we were playing the Grand Theatre. Sue had offered a lift to Eric Shilling, one of the company's principal baritones. He didn't say much during the journey, but the picture of him alighting from the car, pale and shaken, on our arrival in London, will remain for ever in my mind. I couldn't help noticing, though nothing was said, that he did not accept any more lifts from Suzanne.

Carmen was one of the first operas we did, and the Pavilion, Bournemouth, one of our most pleasant dates, especially in June. It was particularly warm that week, and we spent most of our free time on the beach, swimming and sunbathing. One of the advantages of doing this was that it enabled us to avoid the tedious process of applying body make-up, though I can't imagine that our pinkish-brown skin bore much resemblance to the olive complexion of Spanish peasants – however, no adverse comments came from the management. Most of the girls wore little make-up for this opera – just a base and some emphasis on the eyes; we were, after all, only workers in the cigarette factory, and not required to look glamorous. This wouldn't do for Suzanne, though – nothing but the full 'slap' for her, including long luxuriant false eyelashes.

I watched with interest one evening as she put these on. 'Perhaps I should get some of those,' I remarked. 'Of course you should,' replied Suzanne, 'Everyone ought to wear false eyelashes. I'll make you some.' 'What?' I said, astounded, 'How?' 'Easy,' said Sue, and promptly cut a length of coarse black hair from her Carmen wig. She took two large pins from her make-up box and hammered them into the wooden dressing table top with the heel of her shoe, about eight inches apart. She then strung a double line of black thread between them and pulled it taut. I watched, intrigued, as she proceeded to knot on to this, strand by strand, the hair she had taken from the wig. This took quite a while, and we had made several entrances and exits before she had finished this first stage. The next was to trim the hair to suitable eyelash length, then cut the thread into two sections. 'There you are!' said Suzanne. 'Now they just need curling.' She rolled the lashes deftly in paper, fastened it with a pin, and put them in her drawer, 'They'll be ready tomorrow,' she announced.

Some of the other girls had gathered round to watch this unusual procedure. 'Can you make me some?' said one. 'And me!' came several other voices. Soon all the ladies' chorus were wearing Sue's eyelashes at half-a-crown a pair. Some of the principals, seeing how attractive they looked, joined the eyelash queue, and business boomed. Glamour had come to Sadler's Wells, courtesy of Suzanne Steele. Some weeks later, Julie, the wig mistress, came round to collect our *Carmen* wigs for dressing. 'These seem to be getting awfully thin,' she remarked. 'Oh dear,' said Suzanne, sympathetically, 'They don't make things like they used to, do they?' We all fluttered our eyelashes in agreement, but no-one said a word.

Rough working girls we might be in *Carmen*, smoking as we came out of the cigarette factory, (I never liked that bit much, being a non-smoker, and would hurriedly pass mine to a grateful stage hand as soon as we made our exit), but in Anthony Besch's stylish production of Rossini's *La Cenerentola* we were quite the opposite. The opera was exquisitely dressed; we were all courtiers, the girls in magnificent silk crinolines and powdered wigs. I was reminded of my D'Oyly Carte days each time we performed

Cenerentola – in fact Anthony Besch was associated with the Carte several years later when he produced a new *Gondoliers* for them. We stood in an orderly semi-circle with our partners, making conventional gestures; elegance was the keynote. The cast was a strong one: I particularly remember Patricia Kern singing stunningly in the title role, excellently partnered by Kevin Miller as a dashing Prince Ramiro.

Another Besch production was Wagner's *Tannhäuser*. I was quite pleased to be told that I was to appear as one of the sirens at the beginning of the opera, in the Venusberg scene. I was not so pleased when I saw my costume. Over our unflattering pale flesh-coloured tights straggled limp fronds of green nylon seaweed; on our heads we wore the most awful wigs made of what seemed to be long strands of white string. We clung uncomfortably to our rock, arms outstretched, singing and beckoning alluringly to Tannhäuser. 'Come to these bowers!' we entreated seductively. Poor man – after one look at us you would have thought he'd have rushed straight back into the virtuous arms of Elizabeth, which would have shortened the opera considerably. But at least we were behind a gauze, so maybe from the audience we looked slightly more attractive. I was really relieved to change into my plain but elegant dress for the Hall of Song. We entered in a stately procession with our partners, and were seated in an elevated circle – the scene was fairly lengthy, so it was very pleasant to be sitting down. At the end of the opera we put on rough homespun hooded garments to appear as 'younger pilgrims' for that wonderful final chorus. I was singing with all my heart at one performance, when I happened to catch a glimpse of Suzanne, and the sight nearly finished me. All the rest of us, hoping to pass muster as boys, were quite unmade-up, but there she was – in that dreadful shapeless habit, with full stage make-up – eyeshadow, false eyelashes, voluptuous red lips and all. When Sue went on stage, she did it in style.

Humperdinck's *Hansel and Gretel* made its appearance, and I found I was to be one of the fourteen angels in the Evening Prayer sequence, descending a heavenly staircase in a Burne Jones style robe, and clutching a gold palm leaf. This looked quite beautiful from the front, I believe, being most imaginatively lit, and with Humperdinck's sublime music, made a truly unforgettable scene. But that was not all – I had to appear as a 'child' at the end of the opera. All of us 'smaller' girls were cast as children, and as there were sufficient large altos to be our mothers, I suppose the illusion may have been vaguely credible.

One of the bonuses of being a member of an opera chorus is the fact that you quite often have part of an evening – or even a whole evening off. Some of the Mozart and Rossini operas require only a small chorus; in Beethoven's *Fidelio* the girls do not appear until the final triumphant scene, which only lasts for about twenty minutes, but twenty minutes of the most taxing choral singing I have ever been involved in. But whether we happened to be in a particular opera or not, we all had to attend every music call, for choristers had to cover one another and be ready to go on at any time in the event of illness or any other emergency. I remember being 'thrown on' at short notice for another soprano in *Rigoletto* (the absentee was Diana Chadwick, who had been my Alice Fitzwarren in *Dick Whittington*, and who had later joined the Wells). I knew the music, of course, but hadn't much idea of any stage moves. As usual, kind colleagues manoeuvred me into the correct positions with a subtle push or a sly whisper, and I managed pretty well in the circumstances. 'When in doubt, smile' is my maxim in such situations, which is all right if you are doing a happy scene, but rather odd in a tragic one. In the latter case, you may as well revert to your natural feeling of anxiety at being on at all in a piece you don't know. This should produce an anguished expression appropriate to the occasion.

Not long after this I found myself applying a Japanese make-up once more, this time for *Madam Butterfly*. After six years in the D'Oyly Carte this was child's play, and I received many compliments from the other girls. 'Well, I've had quite a bit of practice,' I said modestly – (*How* many *Mikados* had I done?) Our wigs were the usual padded piled-up Japanese style, with a chrysanthemum or two for decoration – after all, we were wedding guests. But there were no long 'Little Maid' braids, and the kimonos had no trains, unlike the D'Oyly Carte ones I had long been accustomed to. This made them easier to manage, but I caught myself on more than one occasion kicking aside a non-existent train, which made me giggle. I really enjoyed *Butterfly*, and there was plenty of scope for some familiar Japanese-type acting in the wedding scene. After the off-stage humming chorus (how difficult it is to hum so high) we were free to go home. *Butterfly* was another of our early nights.

During that 1959 tour we heard some interesting news. *The Merry Widow*, which had been so successful at the Coliseum, was at last to be withdrawn, and another Lehar operetta, *The Land of Smiles*, was to take its place. More importantly,

'T' Company was to replace 'S' Company in this new Coliseum production. The prospect of being in the West End for an indefinite period was an exciting one. We began rehearsals on the new piece; it was full of the glorious melodies so typical of Lehar. I was given the miniscule part of Toni, one of the four adoring girls who gathered round Prince Sou-Chong at a party. He then sang – exquisitely – his Serenade – and we joined briefly in the chorus. I also had a line of dialogue, and at the first rehearsal, as a joke, I said it as one who couldn't pronounce her r's – to my horror the producer, Charles Hickman, liked it, so I was stuck with, 'Oh, I'd love to be cawwied away in a wickshaw' till the end of the run.

At the Coliseum I shared a dressing room with the other three small part girls, one of whom was Suzanne. The others were Rachel Conway and June Johnstone, who was an Australian, and we all got along together pretty well. *The Land of Smiles* was spectacular to look at – you only have to refer to the old vinyl sleeve to get some idea of that – but the plot is hopelessly dated. It deals with the love of Lisa (Elizabeth Fretwell), daughter of a Viennese count, for a Chinese diplomat, Sou-Chong. The unsuitability of such a mixed marriage is barely comprehensible today, but at the turn of the century, when the operetta was set, such a liason was unthinkable. Lisa refutes this prejudice and marries Sou-Chong, accompanying him to China, but when she discovers there are to be four other wives, things don't look quite so rosy. There is a sad subplot, too. Sou-Chong's sister, Mi, (heart-breakingly played by June Bronhill) falls in love with Count Gustl (Peter Grant). There can be no happy outcome for these four characters, and the operetta ends on a rather despairing note, which does not send the audience out in a cheerful frame of mind, unlike the sparkling finale to *The Merry Widow*. On reflection, all the operettas with which I have been involved (and I include Gilbert and Sullivan) seem to end on a happy note, no matter what traumas everyone has been through during the course of the show. 'But, wait –' I hear you say, 'What about *The Yeomen of the Guard*?' Yes, all right, the ending *is* sad, but we have the joy of Elsie and Fairfax to offset the tragedy of Jack Point. And, after all – does he really *die*? Nobody knows for sure, though many have their own opinion on the subject, and various actors have interpreted the final scene as *they* see it. But in *The Land of Smiles* the ending is bleak indeed, as the desolate Sou-Chong, deserted by Lisa, tries to comfort his equally distraught sister, Mi, abandoned in her turn by Count Gustl. At all events, *The Land of Smiles* did not enjoy a long run, and hardly justified the substantial amount of money that had been lavished on it.

In addition to the tiny part of Toni, I was given the second cover to Lisa, becoming the first on matinee days, when the role was played by Estelle Valery. The understudy rehearsals might possibly have brought me to the attention of the management, for I began to make progress from that time, and felt that I had tentatively placed a foot on the bottom rung of the ladder. Houses gradually began to thin out; we wondered what would happen next – whether the show would close, and we would be sent out once again on tour. We needn't have worried though, back came *The Merry Widow* to repeat – or nearly – its former success, and save the situation. Suzanne and I were cast as Grisettes, appearing in Act III Chez Maxim, voluptuously clad in revealing low-necked gowns and black fishnet tights. It goes without saying that Sue's neckline was just that bit lower than anyone else's, the impressive cleavage thus displayed being considerably aided by a pair of rolled-up socks strategically stuffed into her bra. I understudied Valencienne, Baron Zeta's wife, who flirts outrageously with Camille de Rosillon behind her husband's back, only to remind him that she is 'a highly respectable wife' in that most enjoyable duet. I remember one understudy rehearsal when the cover for the Widow had not turned up, and we were having some difficulty with the vocal ensemble. It so happened that June Bronhill had popped in to collect something from her dressing room, and seeing what was going on, came and sang the whole rehearsal with us. She wasn't in the least bothered that she'd have to sing the whole thing again that night – that's what I call a pro! And she was one of the few sopranos I have ever met who could sing a top E flat at ten o'clock in the morning.

Eventually we left the Coliseum and were out on the road once more when a very pleasant event occurred – it was the arrival of my dear friend John Fryatt from the D'Oyly Carte to join the Wells. I had been urging him to do this for some time; I felt that his particular talents would be better realised in a wider theatrical field, which indeed has been the case, for John has since performed many of the operatic character tenor roles, to which he is so well suited, all over the world. He had done well enough in the Carte, playing many principal roles as an understudy, and several others in his own right. He succeeded Thomas Round as Hilarion in the 1954 revival of *Princess Ida*, and regularly played the Defendant in *Trial by Jury*, and Luiz in *The Gondoliers*. On his very last evening with the D'Oyly Carte, not only did he play his usual role as the Defendant in *Trial*, but owing to the indisposition of the principal, he also sang Frederic in *The Pirates of Penzance*, which completed the double bill. Quite a marathon. When the curtain finally came down, Jean Hindmarsh, who had been playing Mabel, stopped him on his way off stage to give him some 'notes' on the performance. 'Oh, by the way, John,' she said, 'The next time you do this –' 'There won't *be* a next time,' replied John, wiping his brow. 'I'm off to Sadler's Wells!'

5.

It seemed that John had made his move to Sadler's Wells at just the right time, for in the spring of 1960, fired by their success with operetta, the management turned their attention to Offenbach. The inimitable Wendy Toye arrived on the scene to produce *Orpheus in the Underworld*, with Alexander Faris to conduct, and Malcolm Pride to design some of his wittiest sets and costumes. We sat in rows in the opera rehearsal room for the read-through; an illustrious cast had been assembled. Kevin Miller was to play the title role, with June Bronhill as his wife, Eurydice, Anna Pollak as Calliope, his formidable mother, and Eric Shilling as Jupiter. These were just a few among the impressive line-up of principals. I found myself with the small part of Aurora, Goddess of Dawn; it was nothing much on paper, but the amusing business I was given to do made it a very rewarding one.

The curtain rose on Act II to reveal (with well-orchestrated snores) the gods and goddesses fast asleep on their clouds on the dizzy heights of Mount Olympus. Several more of these exalted beings crept stealthily on one by one, having been out for a night on the tiles, and anxious not to wake Father Jupiter and incur his wrath. Dry ice (one of my favourite theatrical devices) swirled around in abundance, giving a truly heavenly effect. On a given cue, Aurora, clad in a dawn pink gown of finely pleated chiffon and a long string of pearls – an outfit reminiscent of the 1920s – stretched, yawned, got off her cloud and stomped wearily downstage – (she had, after all, done this every day since time immemorial). With a practised gesture she pulled a cord on her left boob, whereupon her gold sunburst head-dress lit up – as did the stage – and dawn had arrived. I always enjoyed that moment – so, apparently, did the audience. A couple of lines of dialogue were all that remained of the role, but the whole show was great fun, and I loved it.

As for Suzanne – she was cast as Diana, the chaste goddess, and for this role Malcolm Pride had dressed her in scarlet. Originally her tunic of pleated chiffon had been knee-length, but she was not at all happy with this. She considered it unflattering, so out came the scissors, and I swear that dress grew shorter at each performance till she had it just where she wanted it, which was right up to – well, I'll leave that to your imagination. Sue had several nice bits to sing, which she did very well, and made the most of what was in reality quite a small part. All the goddesses were beautifully and imaginatively dressed, and we were individually fitted with flesh-coloured elastic corselettes by Roussel, over which the flimsiest of garments floated gracefully. Our wigs were Grecian in style, of manmade fibre intricately laced with pearls – in fact there were pearls just about everywhere. The gods were rather plainer, with laurel wreaths and draped robes of red or white, and they wore sandals, while the girls had the most beautiful high-heeled satin boots. John Fryatt was, in the beginning, just in the chorus, but later went on to play Mercury, and finally Orpheus himself. I was to be the cover for Calliope, which was quite exciting, for on the pre-London tour Anna Pollak was unavailable the second week. That would be at the Grand Theatre, Leeds, which meant that I would be playing Calliope for the whole week – quite a challenge, for we were all still feeling our feet and only just getting used to our own parts in the show.

Wendy Toye is a remarkable, and in my opinion, a unique lady. She could keep an opera chorus in order like no-one else I know, and, should attention wander, put two fingers in her mouth and emit an ear-splitting whistle. But – even more impressive – she knew everybody's name right from the very beginning of rehearsals. She quickly won over those who would have preferred to be engaged in the solemnity of Wagner to the frivolity of Offenbach, and had the rare knack of making every member of the chorus feel that they were indispensable to the production. Everybody (and opera choruses are not an easy bunch to win over) loved Wendy.

June Bronhill was sensational as Eurydice, playing the role with exactly the right zany humour, and of course singing divinely. Kevin Miller played her priggish husband to perfection, miming his violin playing impeccably as he regaled his wife incessantly with his boring compositions. The whole cast entered into the spirit of the piece wholeheartedly, and right from the outset we knew we had a success on our hands. We opened at Brighton at the beginning of our brief tour before four weeks at the Wells. I remember that first performance vividly; it was very warm, and we stood outside the Hippodrome in a state of great agitation – the half-hour was being called, and no wigs had arrived. Then in the nick of time a van drew up, and there they were. We formed a conveyor belt, passing the wig boxes along the line and in at the stage door. All were safely distributed, then it was panic stations as we rushed to get ready.

Act I took place in a cornfield, with Orpheus's music academy 'The Orpheum' to one side. John and I were two of his dreadful pupils; there were six 'boys' and six 'girls'. The boys had to enter on their knees, wearing thick knee pads which were fitted with shoes; their long white gowns hid the fact that they were kneeling, and they looked like a cross between grotesque children and strange dwarfs. The girl pupils stood behind them as they formed a group, our crazy wigs moving in time to the music as we 'played' execrably on our violins and sang in squeaky voices a farewell to our beloved professor. He was off to Mount Olympus, having been urged by his domineering mother to seek help from the gods to find Eurydice; she had been abducted by Pluto (Jon Weaving), masquerading as Aristaeus, a beekeeper. Everything in Act I was blue and white; we pupils wore white gowns, blue wigs and carried blue violins. The chorus of shepherds and shepherdesses were dressed in white smocks and wigs. Orpheus's tunic was white, finely striped with music staves, and here Malcolm Pride's comic touches were quite brilliant. Perched on Orpheus's shoulder were two birds wearing blue and white striped woolly sweaters, and as he played his violin they nodded and swayed for all the world as if they were enjoying his music. There were many little touches like this on costumes and sets which echoed the humour and spirit of the piece, and helped to make it the remarkable production that it was.

As for Calliope – all her costumes were breathtakingly elegant and a delight to wear, as I found out later, when I took over the role. At the beginning of Act I she enters to do a wonderful prologue straight to the audience, putting them in the picture regarding her daughter-in-law, whom she dislikes very much, and giving them a resumé of the Orpheus legend, until the impatient tapping of the conductor's baton brings her to a halt. Her costume for this act consisted of a blue gown with white polka dots, tight at the knee, then flaring out, a long diaphanous scarf – white with blue spots – drifting from the shoulders. Her chic high-heeled satin boots matched the dress, and her Grecian head-dress, worn over an elegantly coiffured auburn wig – was again white with blue spots. We have not yet finished with polka dots! Calliope carried a cup and saucer (white with blue spots) and a long cigarette holder (blue with white spots). However amazing this ensemble sounds, the overall effect was supremely stylish, and of course fitted in to the blue and white decor of the first act.

In Act II we see Orpheus, Calliope and a chauffeur in a balloon on the way up to Mount Olympus. It amuses me to recall that the part of the chauffeur in this balloon trio was at one time played by Richard Van Allan, who has since become an international star in the world of grand opera. But he is not above reminding me that he was once my chauffeur if we happen to meet! For this number Calliope wore a green and gold creation, with an elaborate feathered head-dress, long green gloves, and carried gold binoculars. Naturally she changed her dress before meeting the gods on Mount Olympus, and Malcolm Pride came up with a marvellous idea for this. Calliope entered downstage right, and Juno came forward to greet her. They met centre stage, turned to each other, and lo – they are wearing identical outfits! Juno's is rose pink and Calliope's turquoise blue, but the elaborate styles are unmistakably the same in every detail. What a laugh this got from the audience!

The third, and final act takes place in Hades, and it is quite near the end when Orpheus and his mother appear, just after the famous can-can. Calliope is again dressed to kill, in a figure-hugging black creation slit up one side to reveal a slim, jet-trimmed trouser leg and long black satin boots. A stole of black (fake) mink, broad brimmed hat and long black gloves completed this eccentric but incredibly sophisticated ensemble.

Looking back over the many years of my stage career, I believe that Calliope was my favourite role, though several others come a very close second. It seems by what I have just said that maybe her costumes might have played a part in that decision! Perhaps they had a slight influence, but it was really the character itself that appealed to me so much. Originally there was no such role as Orpheus's mother, this part being known as Public Opinion. Geoffrey Dunn, who wrote the wonderfully witty script, had the brilliant idea of changing this to the matriarchal figure of Calliope. Her prologue reveals her relationship with her son and her antipathy towards her daughter-in-law in the most amusing way, and she is always ready with an acid comment or a withering glance. I loved every minute of it.

Strangely enough, *Orpheus* didn't get a particularly good press when it opened, but the audiences couldn't get enough of it. Nobody cared much about what the critics said – what the box office said was more to the point. The show was without doubt the most enormous success, and countless revivals were staged over the years. Granada TV wanted it, so we all went off to their studios in Manchester to film a shortened version. Poor John Fryatt, who was to have played

Mercury, slipped on some dry ice and had to be taken to hospital, where it was discovered that he had broken his ankle. He was of course unable to continue filming, but typically made light of his disappointment, returning with his leg in plaster, and regaling us with stories of the casualty department's amazement at the appearance of a bronzed Greek god in a short tunic and winged sandals.

Rather like the Gilbert and Sullivan operas, *Orpheus in the Underworld* has tended to dog my footsteps over the years – not that I'm complaining. An example of this occurred much later, at a time when jobs seemed to be thin on the ground, so I auditioned for extra chorus at the Royal Opera House. This was ad hoc work, spasmodic in nature, and extras were called to augment the regular singers when larger choruses were required. I was accepted, and my first call was for *Fidelio*. This was an opera I knew very well, but only in the English translation, and of course the original German version was used at Covent Garden, so I set to work to learn it at once. I had done one performance (with Klemperer conducting) when a message came from Stephen Arlen at the Wells. 'Whatever are you doing *there*? We need you for *Orpheus* – there's to be another revival!' So with a bit of managerial intervention I was spirited away from the Royal Opera House, back to the Wells. On another occasion, just as I was comfortably ensconced in *Robert and Elizabeth* at the Lyric, a similar message arrived. This time my extradition was pretty straightforward, as both shows were Wendy Toye's productions. To be in demand like that was very flattering to the ego, but I'm quite sure I was not sought after on account of my vocal abilities. Any mezzo soprano could have *sung* the role of Calliope, but the particular type of comedy and characterisation involved probably made the role more difficult to cast. Needless to say, I returned to the Wells with alacrity, and continued to be a guest singer with them for a number of years.

After the first season of *Orpheus* it was back to normal, and some interesting operas came into the repertoire. One of these was Giordano's *Andrea Chénier* – a poignant story set amid the drama and tragedy of the French revolution, with beautiful, and at times deeply moving music rather reminiscent of Puccini in style. I was given my first operatic role – the Countess de Coigny. I had to sweep on in a great crinoline in Act I and order everyone about – (a few unkind people said it was type-casting). Unfortunately I was guillotined in the first interval, so it was a short show for me. Madeleine, my daughter, was played by Victoria Elliot, and as she was considerably older than I, I'm not sure just how convincing the relationship was – however, make-up and lighting work wonders, as I've found out in later years! John had a small part in Act I as the Abbé, after which he, too, disappeared – presumably in the same tumbril.

During one of 'T' Company's seasons at Sadler's Wells a new production of Stravinsky's *The Rake's Progress* was mounted, produced by Glen Byam Shaw, with Colin Davis conducting, and Alexander Young as Tom Rakewell, Elsie Morrison as Ann Truelove, and Raimund Herrincx as Nick Shadow. The chorus were not involved in the first scene, but Scene 2 is set in a brothel presided over by a formidable Mother Goose (Edith Coates). John was a 'roaring boy' and I a whore, plying my trade in a torn and dirty nightdress – a far cry from my recent role as an aristocrat. I was not involved in the auction scene, my next appearance being in Bedlam, where we all milled about as poor deranged creatures in our filthy rags. For this we had to cover ourselves with dirt. Now, body make-up is a tedious thing to apply, and even worse to remove. I got fed up with this, and hit on the idea of bringing a flower pot of garden soil into the dressing room and daubing myself with this – so easy to wash off, and nice and dirty-looking on stage. The other girls, laboriously applying removing cream at the end of the show, watched with envy as I quickly rinsed off my dirt and was away to the pub across the road before they were anywhere near finished. Soon many of them were dipping into my flower pot, and I was having to bring a larger one.

Verdi made an appearance in our schedule in the shape of *La Traviata*. Again I was given a tiny part as a gypsy fortune teller at Flora's party (Heather Begg). Needless to say, I made the most of this great role, though there is a limit to what you can do with one line. This is another opera where the chorus are finished well before the story reaches its tragic end, but I often stayed to listen to the final scene, in my time sung very movingly by Ava June. In a lighter vein, we inherited *Die Fledermaus* from 'S' Company; it was another Wendy Toye production which had been very successful at the Coliseum. Now it was our turn, and we played it on tour, and also at Sadler's Wells. I was given the role of Ida, Adele's sister, which is small but quite important. Adele was beautifully sung by Marion Studholme, a versatile and delightful artiste, but it was Anna Pollak's portrayal of Prince Orlofsky which remains so vividly in my memory. *Die Fledermaus* is full of Johann Strauss's most joyous melodies, and Wendy's lively production fizzed and sparkled like the champagne so often referred to in the lyrics.

We heard, without enthusiasm, that we were to embark on a brand new production of *Merrie England*. This was to be presented in August 1960, with Dennis Arundel as producer, and sets and costumes by Peter Rice. I'm afraid I find Edward German's score tedious and uninspiring, and the prospect of being a simple peasant, jigging about with all those derry-down-derries was infinitely depressing. And so it proved. After tasting the champagne of *Orpheus* and *Fledermaus* it was like drinking some very flat beer. Anna Pollak characterised the role of Queen Elizabeth magnificently, as one would have expected, though ideally I should have preferred a fuller, deeper vocal quality, especially in her famous song, 'O Peaceful England'. Having said that, when at a later date the part was taken over by a full-bodied mezzo, one realised just how much subtlety Anna had given to her characterisation, and that there is much more to Queen Elizabeth than just singing the notes beautifully.

We jolly townsfolk celebrated May Day with 'Sing a down-a down-a' (what *does* that mean?), hailed the Queen, and generally made merry. But, oh – that dreadful 'fishy' number sung by Wilkins (John Holmes/Dennis Dowling) – 'King Neptune sat on his lonely throne', with all those names of fish endlessly recited and repeated (come back, WSG – all is forgiven), as we danced foolishly round in a long line. The liveliest performance of this dull routine that I can remember is when some wag brought on a kipper and slipped it down one of the girls' blouses; it then proceeded to travel from one unfortunate person to another, causing some very

spirited dancing, and later on, some bitter complaints from
the wardrobe. John was one of the Four Men of Windsor,
and Suzanne took over the May Queen from Ava June on
tour, but I remained dispiritedly in the chorus, longing for
the day of the last performance. There was a point towards
towards the end of Act II when a crowd of us sat round
Herne's Oak; one evening, while appearing to be taking a
great interest in the proceedings, I idly tied the apron strings
of several of the girls in front of me to the tree. When we all
stood to greet the Queen as she entered, these unfortunates
were left struggling helplessly to get up. This caused great
amusement in the immediate vicinity, though not visible to
the audience – I should not have done it if it had been.
Naturally, I stood innocently by, wearing an expression of
mild surprise. I must state firmly that I am not in the habit
of engaging in such tricks on stage, but try as I might, I could
not help being bored with the show, though I did my level
best to conceal it.

I apologise to any devotees of *Merrie England* who may be
reading this; I am merely expressing my own opinion of the
piece. After all, it was given its premiere at the Savoy in 1902,
with many D'Oyly Carte favourites in the cast. Henry Lytton
himself was the Earl of Essex, Walter Passmore appeared as
Wilkins, Robert Evett as Raleigh, and Agnes Fraser as Bessie
Throckmorton. Most impressive of all must have been
Rosina Brandram as Queen Elizabeth – now, *that* must have
been some production! But in spite of the casting of all these
Savoy favourites, *Merrie England* enjoyed a mere four-month
run before going out on tour, returning to the Savoy for a
further fifty-six performances in November, 1902,
presumably as a Christmas attraction. Hardly a runaway
success.

I certainly wasn't the only member of 'T' Company who disliked performing *Merrie England*. During one of our tours, when various operas were being presented, an emergency occurred. After a Saturday matinee – I believe it was at Stratford – it was announced over the tannoy that June Bronhill was ill, and unable to appear that evening in the scheduled performance of *Orpheus in the Underworld* (presumably the understudy was also for some reason unavailable). The announcement went on to say that *Orpheus* would be replaced by *Merrie England*. The shouts of pain and anguish from every dressing room in the theatre could be heard for miles!

6.

After *Merrie England* our return to grand opera was like a breath of fresh air. We were pleased to hear that there was to be a new production of *La Bohème*, designed by Voytek. Unfortunately this turned out to be a lacklustre affair, with dismal sets and even more dismal costumes. It is impossible to destroy such a wonderful opera – the sublime music would always triumph over any adversity, but it really is a pity when it is not given the treatment it deserves. I know everyone is supposed to be desperately poor, but surely Act II should be fairly cheerful. Christmas Eve at the Cafe Momus, with a band, excited children, a toyseller, market stalls and all the gaiety of the season ought, in my opinion, to be a bright interlude in marked contrast to the drabness and poverty of the other scenes. But it wasn't. All was drab and dreary – I suppose in the cause of realism. Poor John Fryatt – he was supposed to be a 'student', and for this he had been issued with a dirty-looking sports jacket, out at the elbows, and reputed to have been bought in Chapel Market, just up the road from the Angel. He regarded the offending garment with extreme distaste. 'I've got a better one at home!' he exclaimed crossly, and henceforth proceeded to wear his own jacket. This was an astute move and proved to be very convenient, for at the end of Act II, not being required for the rest of the opera, he simply strolled off the set and out of the stage door – he only lived a stone's throw from the theatre. I was less fortunate, being needed in Act III to disport myself lewdly and raucously in the tavern before I could depart. After that all the chorus were finished, and I suspect that many of us were at home watching News at Ten before poor Mimi had breathed her last.

Mozart came back into the repertoire with a revival of *The Magic Flute*. We had done *The Marriage of Figaro* in my first year with the Wells, and I had loved it, in spite of being a mere peasant – mind you, there is all the difference in the world between a Mozartian peasant and the Edward German equivalent! For this production of *Flute* we were dressed in traditional Egyptian costume, with the typical black, almost geometrical-style wig. I quite fancied myself in this outfit, and I remember crossing the stage at a dress rehearsal to take up my position (the house tabs were out) when I heard a guffaw from the pit. I looked down in surprise – it was from our conductor, Colin Davis. It seemed he thought I looked more like a character from *Carry on Cleo* than a character from a Mozart masterpiece. When I do try to be serious it doesn't always work.

We heard with much pleasure that Wendy Toye was coming back to us, so was Offenbach. Also Alexander Faris to conduct and Malcolm Pride to design – the team that had so successfully created the Sadler's Wells version of *Orpheus in the Underworld*. This time the operetta was to be *La Vie Parisienne*, with book and lyrics again by Geoffrey Dunn; we looked forward to this new production. When the cast list went up on the board we saw that most of the *Orpheus* principals were prominently featured: June Bronhill was to play Gabrielle, the little glove maker; Jon Weaving and Kevin Miller, the two 'men about town', Raoul and Bobinet respectively; Eric Shilling, the gullible Swedish baron, and Anna Pollak his wife. Very much the mixture as before, with three interesting additions: Suzanne Steele was cast as the beautiful courtesan, Métella; John Fryatt as the flamboyant Brazilian millionaire, and myself as Pauline, a saucy lady's maid. When the show first opened there were three more characters – the Brigadier, sung by John Kentish, and a couple of speaking parts in Act II, for which two actresses had been engaged. All these were later cut. Teething troubles like this do occasionally happen when a new show is launched, till the final format is worked out, and in no way do they reflect on the performers.

John's role as the Brazilian (he doesn't have a name) was a large and important one. His first entrance was in the Gare de l'Ouest scene at the beginning of the show, when he burst on with a crowd of girls and launched straight into what amounts to a patter song. This he proceeded to deliver to the manner born, with impeccable D'Oyly Carte diction. He wore a dazzling matador-style suit for this, in brilliant yellow – quite a scene-stealer. Suzanne's big number came in Act III; she made her entrance – and what an entrance – into the night club and sang a charming, bittersweet waltz song reflecting on the decadent night life of the young men of Paris. It was not just the number, or the way she sang it which so impressed the audience – it was also her sensational appearance. She arrived in a great white satin coat lavishly and boldly embroidered with black beadwork; when the head waiter removed this, her gorgeous crinoline was seen to be exactly the reverse – black, with the identical intricate decoration in white. There was always a gasp from the audience at this point – occasionally applause.

My new role did not compare with those two, but I felt that Pauline was tailor-made for me. I only appeared in Act II, first in my demure flowered cotton maid's outfit, with mob cap, and then – after an impossibly quick change – in the

most enormous primrose satin crinoline, exotically trimmed
with ermine tails, and a huge ostrich feather head-dress. I
and my fellow servants had been talked into borrowing our
mistress's finery (she was conveniently away) by the naughty
Bobinet in order to masquerade as the aristocracy. He and
Raoul had devised some devious scheme to extract money
from the easily-deluded Baron by pretending they had gained
admission for him to a highly-exclusive party, and we
servants were to be the illustrious guests. I've had
considerable experience in wearing crinolines, both in the
D'Oyly Carte and afterwards, how to glide smoothly with
small steps so that the hooped skirt doesn't bounce, and how
to manage it gracefully when sitting down. Now, however, I
had to behave like someone who has never worn a crinoline
before, walking normally, and letting it bounce about in an
uncontrolled way.

I've done some pretty quick changes in my time – from Aunt
Em into the Sorceress of the North (*Wizard of Oz*) during a
couple of lightning flashes and a few rolls of thunder takes
some doing, but I believe Pauline's complicated
transformation from maid into countess was the fastest ever.
As I came off stage, my dresser and the wig mistress were
waiting. The dresser undid my maid's costume and petticoat
and slipped them off while I dealt with the mob cap; she
had laid out my hooped underskirt, and on top of that my
great crinoline, leaving a hole in the middle, where my shoes
were placed. I leapt half-naked into the shoes (no time for
modesty here) then she hauled up the heavy dress and
underskirt, fastening both securely. Meanwhile, the wig
mistress, who was holding a mirror, helped me on with my
head-dress, and pinned it as firmly as she could, while the

dresser handed me my large feather fan, and, pulling on my gloves as I went, I hurried back on stage to greet the Baron.

After we had been introduced, everyone else pointedly withdrew, leaving me to do my worst. The Baron had left his wife at their hotel, with the express purpose of enjoying some Parisian night life, and it was part of the scheme that I should help him to do so. It was obvious that he was very taken with me, and completely fooled by my assumed aristocratic tones. He seated himself on a small bench and invited me to sit beside him. This I did, with a becoming show of reluctance, but being unaccustomed to wearing a crinoline, I gave it a mighty swing as I sat down. I turned to the Baron, but he had vanished; puzzled, I looked around for him, then, lo – he appeared from beneath my layers of petticoats, a lace frill round his face. Much embarrassed, (though *he* didn't seem to mind at all) I hurriedly re-arranged my dress, and our duet, 'Little Cloud' began. This is a delightful number, both sweet and funny, and got a wonderful response from the audience.

The rest of the act gradually turned into a riotous party, with everyone in strangely bizarre costumes. Most of the girls, unaccustomed to their borrowed splendour, had got their dresses on wrong; one was completely back to front, their head-dresses were either precarious or crooked – or both – and one was upside down. Each was announced as some spurious member of the elite, by a name hastily thought up for the occasion. There was, for instance, 'Madame La Comtesse de Laissez Faire' and 'Madame La Baronne de Bête Noir', and among the men, 'General Fracas' and 'Monsieur de Rigeur'. The Baron, being quite unused to

Parisian aristocracy, and not at all fluent in the French language, took all this most seriously, and was duly impressed. The high spot was the appearance of Bobinet in a peculiar naval uniform, far too small for him, declaring himself to be a Swiss admiral. In his effort to get dressed, the back seam of his coat had given way completely, which gave rise to the hilarious ensemble, 'Do you know you're splitting down the back?' Gabrielle and the Brazilian had by then joined the party; she wore the most stunning white crinoline, and looked really beautiful. The Brazilian had for some obscure reason become caught up in the conspiracy, and was strangely attired as an improbable eastern potentate. From then on the party gathered momentum, champagne flowed, and all inhibitions vanished. The action got wilder and wilder, and the curtain finally came down on a scene of inebriated chaos (impeccably sung, of course). The audience loved it, and we ascended the stairs to our dressing rooms, weary but exhilarated. 'Follow that!' we said smugly to our colleagues who had been listening to the laughter and applause over the tannoy, and who were about to begin Act III.

We recorded the highlights of *La Vie Parisienne* at EMI; most of Act II was featured, including the 'Little Cloud' duet with Eric Shilling. I was glad of this, for I had not done well with recordings up till then; there had been none at all during my time as a principal with the D'Oyly Carte. My one-liner as Sacharissa in *Princess Ida* still survives on the old 1955 vinyl recording!

Halfway through 1961 a strange rumour began to filter through to us. The copyright on the Gilbert and Sullivan operas would shortly expire, and there were many dire predictions as to what might happen to them in the future. Then it was confirmed that 'T' Company was to present the first out-of-copyright production of *Iolanthe* on January 1st 1962, and as we would be at the Memorial Theatre, Stratford-on-Avon on that date, that is where the important event would take place. I received the news with mixed feelings; I had not joined the Wells to perform G & S – that part of my life was over – or so I had thought! At the same time I could not help experiencing a sneaking sensation of pleasure at the idea. I then heard that I was to be cast as Leila. That would be a change for me – I'd played Celia and I'd played Phyllis. Frank Hauser, a well-known drama producer, was to direct; it was said that he'd never seen a Gilbert and Sullivan opera. What dreadful things might he do to it, I wondered. Desmond Heeley would design sets and costumes, and I was much relieved to hear that the music would be in the capable hands of Alexander Faris – at least there would be nothing to worry about in that direction.

As it turned out, there was no need for anxiety where Frank Hauser was concerned. He had an instinctive feel for Gilbert's dialogue, and a genuine understanding of the style of the piece. On the whole I approved of what he did, though there were one or two things that I could not accept. Why do so many producers think it hilarious to depict the fairies as clumsy, clodhopping characters in the opening scene? Bored they may be – after all, they have been performing the same old routines for so long; or sad, perhaps, because Iolanthe, who devised these songs and dances is no longer with them – 'We sing her songs and we trip her measures, but we don't enjoy ourselves'. But clumsy – never! Leave

that to the mortals. I'm afraid the Wells fairies made their
entrance in that fashion, which seemed rather at odds with
their dainty dresses. Another innovation which I found
unnecessary and distracting was the introduction of a tearful
peer, who sobbed and boo-hooed loudly at Phyllis's rejection
of the nobility. Apart from these two things, I found little to
criticise.

Frank Hauser was great fun to work with, and had a very
good sense of humour – an essential requisite for any Gilbert
and Sullivan producer. He had an amusing idea for Leila in
the opening dialogue scene. When I said my line, 'But that's
one of the advantages of being immortal – we never grow
old,' he suggested that I should step momentarily out of the
Arcadian landscape and address this line directly to the
audience, while the rest of the fairies 'froze'. The line
delivered, I would step back into the scene, which would
then come to life and proceed. I liked this – so did the
audience. It seemed to make sense, for why should Leila
impart this piece of information to her fellow fairies?
Presumably they have been aware of it since the beginning
of time; even Fleta, who seems to be uninformed as to the
nature of Iolanthe's misdemeanour, must certainly be au fait
with the advantages of fairyhood! A piece of business I was
not so sure about occurred during the Fairy Queen's song
in Act II. When she sang, 'In that we gain a Captain Shaw,'
I had to look up sharply (our heads were bowed at that point),
deeply puzzled as to who this gentleman was. I then nudged
Celia, and mouthed silently, 'Who's Captain Shaw?' She
looked equally mystified, shrugged her shoulders, and
turned round to enquire of the fairy behind. This gathered
momentum, and soon all the fairies were asking one another

the same question – it did get a laugh, but I was never quite sure it should have happened during that lovely song. I did the business as discreetly as I could, but inevitably the laughter came. Heather Begg, who played the Fairy Queen (and an excellent characterisation it was) didn't seem to mind, so it stayed in. I imagine that many principal contraltos would have raised the roof over such a distraction during their song – what *would* Bertha Lewis have said?

Elizabeth Harwood sang Phyllis charmingly, partnered by Julian Moyle as Strephon. It was strange at first to see someone else playing 'my' role, but I concentrated on my own small part, which I certainly enjoyed. Eric Shilling, always good value, had an appropriately wicked sparkle in his eye, and a suitably dry legal tone for the Lord Chancellor. I missed the lightness of touch, impish quality and agility of John Reed, but Eric's vastly different interpretation was perfectly valid. Patricia Kern's beautiful mezzo soprano voice was at its best in Iolanthe's song, which she sang with great pathos, but I must admit I found her more mortal than fairy. There is a particular subtlety needed for the role of Iolanthe – something more than just an excellent voice – and I do believe that Joyce Wright possessed the quality I mean. Judging by evidence I have heard, I am quite certain that Marjorie Eyre had it too.

The two earls were the redoubtable Dennis Dowling (Mountararat) and Stanley Bevan (Tolloller) – until then a chorus member. They made a fine pair – Dennis was an old favourite with Wells audiences, and did great justice to his song in Act II. Leon Greene – yet another ex-D'Oyly Carte singer – played Private Willis. There were actually four of us from the Carte in that production – John Fryatt, Elvet Hughes, Leon Greene and myself.

Desmond Heeley's designs for both sets and costumes were inspired. He devised a fragile spider's web cloth for the opening, which made us all look diminutive and fairylike; this flew out later to reveal an Arcadian landscape. I was amazed when I saw the new D'Oyly Carte production in 1977 to find exactly the same thing happening. Hey, wait a minute – I thought – we did that way back in 1962! Their new fairy costumes, too, bore quite a resemblance to those of the Wells, the latter being dark green and silver, and the Carte's black and silver. But each of our dresses were ornamented with a different flower, one on the shoulder, and a matching spray on the skirt. Mine had butterflies instead of flowers, and Celia's (Elizabeth Robson) silver cobwebs; they really were delightful.

The music was impeccably handled by Alexander Faris – I don't know when I have heard the overture more sensitively played. The orchestra was considerably larger that that employed by the D'Oyly Carte, so obviously it was able to do the beautiful score the justice it deserves.

What I appreciated about the Sadler's Wells *Iolanthe* was that it was treated with great respect, and not trivialised or 'sent up' in any way. For someone who had never seen a Gilbert and Sullivan opera, it was surprising how Frank Hauser retained so many of those traditional qualities that many of us still hold dear. I am by no means in favour of the slavish following of tradition just for the sake of it; I love new ideas, clever innovations and a different approach to familiar situations, but some recent productions fill me with despair. I hear the so-called directors saying, 'Oh, I've got a marvellous idea – let's have one of the Three Little Maids pregnant, and give them funny hats like lampshades, and – oh, I know! Peep-Bo can wear glasses and speak with a lisp – what a scream!' Well, it may be a scream for the production team, but it's yawning time for me. It reveals a complete lack of understanding of the intent of the Savoy operas, and also a serious lack of talent or imagination. All the laughs we need are there in the libretto. If we can't get them without funny hats, we should examine our timing and delivery.

All this reminds me of the last night of Orpheus in the Underworld, when Wendy Toye came round to the dressing rooms to wish us good luck. 'Darlings,' she said, 'Please don't send the show up tonight. All the jokes are there already – if you interfere with them you'll cancel them out, and the fun will be spoiled.' Such was our respect for Wendy that anyone planning to introduce some funny last night business quietly changed their minds and left well alone. Consequently we had a wonderful show, with all the careful timing left undisturbed, and there couldn't have been more laughter and applause. I think this piece of advice applies perfectly to the G&S operas – they just don't need silly walks or funny hats – or any other cheap gimmicks.

The first night of Iolanthe was of course a complete sell-out, yet there were quite a few empty seats. The reason for this was the weather – snow lay thickly on all the roads, and was still falling as the audience arrived. Some of those who managed to get to Stratford were unable to get home. They were forced to find what accommodation they could, and stay the night, for it snowed non-stop throughout the performance, and the roads became pretty well impassable. Luckily most of the cast were staying within walking distance from the theatre; I and a number of my colleagues were, as usual, at the Old Red Lion, just five minutes away. Yet, snowed in as they were, the audience seemed to enjoy the show immensely. Laughter and applause came when they should, and we felt that the first out-of-copyright G&S opera was a success. We were pleased for Frank Hauser, for Sandy Faris and for Desmond Heeley. Most of all we were pleased for Gilbert and Sullivan – I think they might have approved.

7.

And so life went on. Our tours were interspersed with welcome seasons at Sadler's Wells, and I took over the role of Calliope in *Orpheus*, which was very gratifying. That, with Pauline, Leila and Ida meant that I was seldom just singing in the chorus, though not actually a principal. I was in fact in a rather unusual position; operetta was obviously my forte, but it was naturally a relatively small part of the Wells repertoire. To give the management their due, I was given every opportunity possible; whenever operetta was on the agenda I found myself with a rewarding role to play. Grand opera was another thing altogether.

We had said goodbye to the successful *Merry Widow*; by arrangement with the Australian impresario Garnet Carroll, the whole production, headed by June Bronhill and several other major principals, had been shipped over to Australia, together with staff producer, conductor William Reid, and all the sets, costumes and props. It had done excellent business over there, and there was a rumour – just a slight one – that *Orpheus* might also be destined for the Antipodes. The rumour grew stronger; we wondered who would go – would they want the original cast? They couldn't have June Bronhill as Eurydice – she was still over there, and having finished with *Merry Widow*, was just about to open as Maria in *The Sound of Music*. Meanwhile, Iris Kells had taken over Eurydice, and had been playing it for some time. And would they want Anna Pollak? After all, she created the role of Calliope; I lost quite a bit of sleep, wondering what would be the outcome.

While all this was going on, 'T' Company were putting on a new production of *The Bartered Bride* (Smetana), produced by Pauline Grant. Oh dear, I anguished – more jolly peasants – Czechoslovakian ones this time, but it made no difference –

> 'Now's the time for fun and jollity –
> We shall have a holiday, a holiday'

we sang, dancing in circles and trying to look enthusiastic. I hated it, of course but when I saw a performance of the opera many years later, I enjoyed it thoroughly.

At last the news broke. Yes – *Orpheus* was indeed bound for the Antipodes, and I was invited to go. Iris Kells, Eric Shilling (Jupiter), Kevin Miller (Orpheus), Jon Weaving (Pluto), John Fryatt (Mercury – also covering Orpheus, with a view to an eventual take-over), and Suzanne Steele (Diana) were to be my companions, with Robert Blake to re-stage the show, and Alexander Faris to conduct. The rest of the company – small parts and chorus – would be cast in Australia, and would have learned the show by the time we arrived to begin rehearsals. Pat Bancroft, who had been 'T' company manager for some time, was to accompany us in that capacity. The trip was an exciting prospect; most of the principals were to fly; John and I agreed to go by ship – we had time to do this, and thought it would be an enjoyable and relaxing way to travel, but alas – family matters compelled me to remain in England until the last possible moment, so John had to set off alone, while I flew out with the others at a much later date. Iris Kells announced that she proposed to break her journey and spend a couple of days in Delhi, where she had spent part of her childhood. This seemed a good idea to me, so I volunteered to accompany her, and we then decided that additional stopovers in Athens and Cairo would be very worthwhile. We set off from Heathrow in an Alitalia Comet, parting company with Eric Shilling and his wife, Erica Johns, at Rome airport. Erica was also a singer, and although not a member of Sadler's Wells, was accompanying her husband on the trip, and was to play Cupid – a small part which she did very well.

Athens was, it goes without saying, all we had expected. In those days – 1962 – access to the Acropolis was unrestricted, and we were able to examine the whole site in detail, and at close hand, which was an unforgettable experience. Something more mundane, and eminently forgettable, however, was the dish of octopus I foolishly sampled in a slightly dubious cafe; the rather uncomfortable effects slightly inhibited my enjoyment of the next few days!

Cairo was another remarkable stop, and Iris and I packed all we possibly could into our brief visit. The things we did – visiting the soukh, the Tutankhamun exhibition, riding on camels to visit the Sphinx and the Pyramids of Giza – are fairly commonplace today, but in 1962, when overseas tourism was still in its infancy, such adventures were relatively novel, and certainly exciting.

After a brief stop in Bombay, we arrived in the sweltering and humid heat of Delhi, where we collapsed for a short interval before setting out to see as much as possible. Jolting over the rough streets in a bicycle-driven rickshaw did not help my still-delicate digestion, but I doggedly pointed my camera at all the right things, and marvelled at the sights and sounds (and smells!) of that great city. Then – at last –

Australia awaited us; after calling at Darwin the next and final stop would be our destination – Sydney.

I felt at home the moment I stepped on to Australian soil. The first thing I remember is a wonderful cup of 'white tea' – I shall never taste a better one. The press was waiting for us, together with management representatives, and we certainly needed the extra layer of make-up we had hastily applied before landing. As soon as we could, we were off to our arranged accommodation to catch up on sleep before rehearsals began in a couple of days time.

Austalians are notably a friendly lot, and the *Orpheus* cast were no exception. We were welcomed warmly, and rehearsals began in a happy and co-operative atmosphere. We found everyone keen to acquire the necessary style of the piece, and there was certainly plenty of talent and vitality; soon the production was shaping up nicely for the first night at the Tivoli Theatre on August 17th, 1962.

During the rehearsal period, with evenings free, we were able to sample some of the shows currently running in Sydney. Two in particular spring to mind: *Sentimental Bloke* and *Once upon a Matttress*. The former was based on the poems of CJ Dennis, and very funny indeed; I particularly enjoyed the raucous character played by Gloria Dawn, surely one of Australia's best comedy actresses. But soon our free evenings came to an end, and we were to begin our eight shows a week season at the Tivoli. The first night was a wonderful occasion, and the response all we could have wished for. The critics, too, were enthusiastic, though one or two were not altogether without a few reservations. One, Lorna Curtin, wrote in *Theatregoer* magazine:

'I cannot join the chorus of undiluted approbation for this production. Perhaps I'm just cross-grained. Not, of course, that there wasn't a great deal to evoke lavish praise; the heavenly costumes and diabolically clever sets should be a source of much *pride* to their designer.' (Oh, the puns!) 'The orchestra, under Alexander Faris, handled Offenbach's coruscating music with musicianly skill rarely heard here in comic opera; in Iris Kells we had an Eurydice who had The Lot (attractive voice, sufficient acting ability, pretty face, and a nice pair of legs which she displayed to advantage in the bath scene).' Then the critic goes on to admire the mechanics of the production, in which she finds no fault. Next she proceeds to object strongly to the 'embarrassingly unfunny Orpheus pupils', and the 'laborious underlining of references to heaven, hell and gods' and continues:

'Finally, there was a surfeit of waggling bottoms, which are very well in moderation. Even Eurydice had to bend down, backside towards Jupiter, so that he could say, "You're even more adorable than I imagined". I'd be interested to know if the fun was laid on with a trowel specially for Australian consumption' (that was certainly *not* the case) 'or am I hypersensitive on this subject? After two paragraphs of gripes, back to the credit list. Cynthia Morey as Calliope has the requisite dry wit and sense of style, and Eric Shilling's Jupiter was delightful. Gordon Wilcox (an Australian) sang richly and movingly as John Styx, and Suzanne Steele looked and sounded delicious as Diana.' I think that was probably the worst write-up we ever got!

Most of us remained in our temporary accommodation till we had become accustomed to the differences in time and climate, then set out to find more independent places to stay for our six week season in Sydney. I would normally have shared with Suzanne, but her complicated love life rather got in the way!

After looking around different areas I found a suitable apartment in Elizabeth Bay; it was quite large, so I invited John and Kevin Miller to share it. This arrangement worked well; we all took turns with the cooking, and although it was quite a walk, we often found time to return home between shows on matinee days. A funny incident springs to mind: At one point in the show the gods and goddesses sang a chorus of thanks to Father Jupiter: 'Praise him loud, and praise him well'. They had been lectured about their diction, and told to make more of the consonants 'PR' in 'praise'. The consequence of this was that the word sounded more like '<u>B</u>raise'. That afternoon, during the matinee, we got to that chorus, and as I heard them singing what sounded like '<u>B</u>raise' him loud' etc I remembered that we'd left a casserole in the oven back at the flat, intending to turn it off before we left for the matinee – had anyone done so? I certainly hadn't. Being next to Kevin on stage, I was able to murmur, sotto voce, 'Did you turn off the oven?' He looked at me in dismay, and answered in the negative. On the soonest possible occasion, he manoeuvred himself near to John, and asked the same question, he received a horrified 'No!' We did the rest of Act II finale in a state of anxiety, until we could get to a telephone and contact someone. I think we eventually managed to get in touch with the cleaning lady, who kindly went and turned off the gas. So our supper was saved, but I never heard that particular chorus again without a smile.

Sydney was a wonderful place to be; although it was winter, I found it as warm as a good English summer. I surprised the Australian members of the cast, who considered it cold, by swimming at Bondi beach – the sea was certainly warmer than in England in high summer. The only trouble with Australia was that there were an alarming number of parties nearly every night – I confess I went to rather a lot of them, but then my role in *Orpheus* did not demand high lyrical singing, otherwise I should have had to be much more careful, and look after my voice. Once the show was running, there was time for leisure pursuits, and the three of us flatmates took up painting. There were some remarkable results, and one day we turned the apartment into an art gallery, which of course meant another party so that the bemused guests could look at our masterpieces. We were invited to numerous events and excursions, and before we knew where we were, it was time to leave lovely Sydney for Melbourne and the Princess Theatre.

Our season in Melbourne opened on September 26th, to much the same level of appreciation as in Sydney, and we seemed to be all set for a successful run. I did not like the city nearly as well, in spite of the wide streets, gracious buildings and abundance of palm trees. The people seemed rather different – more reserved than in Sydney, and less inclined to be friendly. I found a flatlet in a very pleasant complex within walking distance of the theatre, and was intrigued to find a heavily-laden lemon tree outside my window. Melbourne's climate seemed to be very capricious;

one day the temperature rose to nearly 100°F – the next it was only 45°, with a strong wind. I missed the consistent sunshine and blue skies of Sydney. Iris and I had communicating dressing rooms at the Princess, and shared a dresser by the name of Doris. She was absolutely hopeless – never there when needed, and when she did turn up in time for a change could never seem to match a hook with its corresponding eye. We usually ended up by dressing each other. The trouble was – Doris was such a dear that we felt we had to put up with her, and still gave her a big tip at the end of each week just for being nice!

As the year drew towards its end we faced the prospect of going with *Orpheus* to New Zealand, and were given the option of extending our contracts to cover a tour of four cities – Auckland, Palmerston North, Wellington and Christchurch. Iris Kells, Kevin Miller, Eric Shilling and his wife all elected to return to England; the rest of us felt that the opportunity of visiting New Zealand was too good to miss, so at the end of our ten week season in Melbourne we said goodbye to our departing colleagues and flew to Auckland in a Lockheed Electra, arriving just before Christmas. Pat Bancroft and I found a very nice flat owned by the president of the local water ski-ing club, with the result that we were soon skimming across Auckland Bay behind his motor boat (or more or less!). What a scramble it was to get enough provisions in time for the extended holiday period, which we discovered lasted for two weeks. I remember being amazed and most annoyed at everything closing down for so long, but nowadays it seems that it's just as bad over here – at least it was summer in New Zealand, which seemed to make more sense.

With some of the major principals returning home, there had to be several cast changes. Suzanne moved up into the role of Eurydice, John Fryatt was now to play Orpheus, and Gordon Wilcock, the Australian who had been singing John Styx, the King of the Boeotians, took over the much larger part of Jupiter. The roles left vacant by this re-casting were now to be filled by Australians. Alexander Faris remained to preside over the music, and Robert Blake stayed for a brief time to re-stage the show. It seemed quite odd to see unfamiliar people in the roles we knew so well, but we soon adapted to the changes, and *Orpheus* opened at Her Majesty's Theatre, Auckland, on the 21st January 1963.

I don't think the New Zealand audiences were quite ready for *Orpheus* in those days. The vista of apparently half-naked goddesses disporting themselves riotously on the stage, and Eurydice in a bubble bath, together with some rather risqué dialogue evoked a certain amount of disapproval from the press. Apparently the management took note of this, for *The Merry Widow* was brought in to run in conjunction with *Orpheus*. Casting for this was obvious: Suzanne would play Anna Glavari, the Widow; Jon Weaving, Danilo; John Fryatt, Camille; myself, Valencienne, with Gordon Wilcock as my husband, Baron Zeta. Again, Australian singers would fill the smaller roles. It was good to have two shows on the go, and I had always loved the *Widow*. Only one member of the cast was not pleased – that was John. He had never really enjoyed romantic roles, though he could certainly sing them; he felt much more at ease with comedy, and with his excellent sense of timing, excelled in that field. Camille was too sentimental for his liking. We had two duets – the first, 'A Highly Respectable Wife' was most enjoyable to sing, but the one in Act III – the summerhouse duet – was highly romantic, and sometimes when we gazed soulfully into each other's eyes the urge to giggle was almost irresistible. We did not give way to this weakness, I hasten to add, but were often quite relieved to escape into the summerhouse at the end of the duet. Here, I have to confess to the occasional bit of mischief; Gordon Wilcock, as Baron Zeta then had to creep up to the summerhouse door and peer between the slats – what he saw inside I am not prepared to reveal in these pages, but he had a lot of dialogue to get through with a straight face while viewing what went on within!

Auckland is a beautiful city – at least, so it was in 1963, and I do hope modern buildings have not spoiled it too much. The backdrop of Rangitoto, the extinct volcano, (upon which we spent most of Christmas Day) and the wide blue bay provide a lovely setting. As well as working hard, we were able to enjoy many excursions, the most memorable being a trip to Rotorua to see the geysers and the extraordinary pools of boiling mud. The Maori settlement, with a genuine demonstration of the Haka (war dance) and the sweet sound of a Maori choir singing in perfect harmony remain vividly in my memory. There were many other adventures, too; when the Queen visited Auckland, our kind landlord and his wife took Pat and me out into the bay in their boat at crack of dawn to welcome the royal yacht Britannia – there we were, with literally hundreds of small craft, every one dressed overall, and sounding sirens and whistles and anything that would make a noise. There was barely room for the Britannia to make her way through, and I should imagine the royal party were very touched by this warm reception. As previously mentioned, water ski-ing was a great attraction; there was much falling in at first, but who cared when the sea was as warm as a tepid bath?

Palmerston North, our next venue, was quite another kettle of fish – (where have I heard that expression before?). For one thing it was inland, and we missed the exhilarating maritime freshness of Auckland. We just could not believe the hotel when we arrived – we felt we had stepped back a hundred years and had been dropped into the middle of a set for a Western. Our rooms were primitive in the extreme, and on going down into the dining room – a sort of saloon – we were offered hogget and silver beet. Having accepted this unfamiliar dish we found it was actually lamb with a type of spinach – I did not much care for it. The greatest shock was when a terrific noise shook the flimsy building, accompanied by the loud clanging of a bell – it was a train thundering past. The railway went right through the centre of the town, and we discovered that this was not called the Central Hotel for nothing. The track was just outside our bedroom windows. What if this happens all through the night, we wondered – but luckily there didn't seem to be too many trains during the small hours, and a large gin and Fanta – a fairly obnoxious fizzy drink – (we could not get any tonic) proved a useful nightcap.

The Opera House turned out, not unexpectedly, to be a rather basic venue, but the response from the audience for the *Widow* left nothing to be desired – as expressed in the press coverage: 'Palmerston North audiences are not usually noisily demonstrative, so the stamping through many of the curtain calls at last night's performance of *The Merry Widow* could be taken by the company as local appreciation of the highest order.' For the benefit of any D'Oyly Carte faithfuls who may be reading this, I will quote another excerpt from the same review, so that they will know that John and I were maintaining the old standards: 'Two performances of particular appeal were those of Cynthia Morey, the ambassador's wife, and John Fryatt as Camille de Rosillon, the French diplomat. In their several scenes together the voices of these two blended perfectly, and they maintained the air of quality that permeated the whole performance.' So you see, we were not giggling *all* the time!

Wellington was our next stop, and an enjoyable one, too. Five of us rented a very nice house perched up on the cliff, overlooking the sea. Pat Bancroft, Pam Fasso (an Australian singer playing Diana), John and I occupied the bedrooms, while Sandy Faris luxuriated in the sun lounge, into which he immediately moved a large hi-fi and proceeded to play opera and classical music into the small hours, causing some annoyance among those trying to sleep. I found a wonderful solution, however – I followed a friend's recommendation and bought some very effective earplugs from the Para Rubber Company, so was quite unaffected by the nightly sun lounge symphony concerts! But we all got along together very well on the whole, and our stay in Wellington proved both successful and enjoyable.

Just before we left, I was delighted to receive a call from NZBC asking if John and I would be prepared to do a programme for them, to go out on CHTV (Christchurch) on April 8th. Now, what shall we sing? I pondered, visions of songs from operetta and musicals filling my head, together with ideas for staging and presentation. 'We want Gilbert and Sullivan, of course,' said the powers-that-be, 'a discussion of the operas, reminiscences, and a few songs and duets.' And I had thought I'd escaped from all that – how much farther from the Savoy can you get than 12,000 miles? So off to the studio we went, gave them exactly as they wanted, and sang excerpts from *The Mikado*, *The Gondoliers*, *Ruddigore*, and *Patience*. And we had to admit we enjoyed it.

From Wellington, the last date on the North Island, to Christchurch, way down south. What a lovely city – elegant buildings, an attractive feeling of space and tranquility, and a decidedly Scottish air. Autumn was approaching, and although the weather was fair, it was becoming rather cool. Some of us hired bicycles, which we found most convenient for getting about, as the country was very flat. The shows were well appreciated, but we began to have an end-of-tour feeling, and even a touch of homesickness after so long away. The tour was continuing – I believe it was to go to Tasmania, and up into Queensland, but though the prospect was tempting, the lure of home was stronger. Sue and Jon Weaving decided to stay on, but Sandy, John and I, having made up our minds to leave, agreed that we must make the most of our journey home, and talked over the various possibilities. We eventually chose to spend a few days in Fiji, Honolulu, San Francisco and New York, and on April 16th we left New Zealand, seen off exuberantly at the airport by members of the cast – it was quite a sad occasion. Needless to say, our long trip back was an unforgettable experience, with scenic beauty in Fiji, sun and surf in Honolulu, meeting old friends in San Francisco, and theatregoing and shopping in New York. Then it was back to London – and we were home at last.

8.

Sitting at the kitchen table, eating cornflakes at 3am, (my internal clock being at sixes and sevens) I wondered what I would do next. The first thing of course was to visit my family and regale them with my Antipodean adventures (or *some* of them!) This I did, after which it was time to think about work. There was nothing for me at the Wells just then, operetta temporarily having taken a back seat, so I must look elsewhere. I did not feel quite the same urgency to find a job as in my pre-Wells days, for I had been earning good money for a long time, and felt relatively affluent after my recent tour. So I did not rush to become a waitress or an usherette! Luckily, those days were over. Two or three concerts saw me through the summer, and at the end of August I heard that the Players' Theatre was putting on a musical called *House of Cards*; apparently it had been presented at the Players' for a four-week season in January that year, and now the management were to put it on at Wimbledon Theatre and Golders Green before a West End transfer to the Phoenix Theatre. This sounded an interesting project, so I auditioned and was accepted, though in rather a minor capacity.

My reasons for accepting the contract were twofold; first and foremost, it was time I found some work, and secondly, I was keen to find a way into the Players' Theatre – that tiny, elite institution tucked away under the arches in Villiers Street, just off the Strand, where so many celebrities have made their debut. More about the Players' later. Peter Greenwell, who often presided at the piano there, had written the book and music for *House of Cards*, and Peter Wildeblood, the lyrics. The show was based on a story by

Ostrovsky, which, on the face of it, does not seem to be very likely material for a West End success. Vida Hope, who had been responsible for *The Boy Friend* (also originally a Players' production) was to direct, and Reggie Woolley to design sets and costumes. I found myself cast as Madame Vyroubova (an aristocrat) and – at the other end of the scale – the Cook! The time was just before the Russian revolution.

Rehearsals were congenial; Peter Greenwell's music was interesting and tuneful. I didn't have a lot to do, but enjoyed what I did. Costumes were splendid – as, I found out later, was always the case with anything to do with the Players' – and there were many original and authentic accessories and props. But the show itself just did not work – two weeks pre-West End, and four weeks at the Phoenix were all that could be managed, and it had to close. But I met some very interesting people – there was a young girl called Ruth Llewellyn in my dressing room – she made her name later as Ruth Madoc, of *Hi-de-Hi* fame. Another actor in *House of Cards* who subsequently achieved much success was 23-year-old Patrick Mower, straight from RADA. And I had achieved the object of the exercise: I was invited to be in the Players' pantomime that Christmas.

During the year the Players' present an old time music hall bill that changes once a fortnight. The establishment is a theatre club, and patrons are required to be members to gain admission. Drinks are served before, during and after the show; there is a supper room which operates until quite late, and a bar which is open till midnight. Some years ago, owing to re-development, the theatre moved higher up Villiers Street, and is now much smarter, though I don't feel it has quite the same atmosphere as the old 'pink tunnel'. We called it that because the long narrow auditorium was painted a fairly hideous shrimp colour. After the show, when we had changed, we had to cross the stage and go through the audience to leave by the front of house. There was no other way, except a dismal ill-lit alley where many unspeakable dangers probably lurked, and which was only used in the direst of emergencies (such as fire, or turning up late for the performance!) And as the bar was at the back of the auditorium, we often didn't get much farther than that! Not that we minded – it was quite nice to chat to members of the audience en route.

My first Players' pantomime, *The Sleeping Beauty in the Wood*, was a revelation, and completely different from the others I had done. For one thing, it was faithfully and traditionally Victorian, with the original script of 1840, by J.R. Planché. A few lyrics and odd bits of dialogue had been added, but very little, and the music was classical or traditional. Wit and dreadful puns abounded, and the whole thing was meticulously directed and polished by Don Gemmell. He and Reggie Woolley (who designed the sets and costumes) were co-directors of the Players' Theatre.

When I first stepped on to that tiny stage – no bigger than your average living room – I couldn't imagine how on earth any show could be put on there, never mind a pantomime. But Reggie's sets were quite amazing: fairy landscapes, baronial halls and impressive castles appeared out of nowhere, magically painted and lit. The costumes were just as brilliant, Victorian in design of course, often with genuine period additions, and wondrous head-dresses, crowns and wands – the whole thing looked magnificent. I was glad to be part of it, though in my first Players' panto I was only the Princess's nurse!

Dress rehearsals were always special. The entire cast was entertained to a lavish spread in the supper room during the interval, with enough wine to ensure plenty of vitality in Act II! Many of the Players' stalwarts featured in the leading roles – Joan Sterndale Bennett, Sheila Bernette and John Rutland among them. Geoffrey Brawn was responsible for the musical arrangements, and 'presided at the Grand Pianoforte'. He was painstaking in his efforts to get the ensembles really good – not an easy job, as the music used was sometimes quite difficult, and a fair number of participants were actors! However, there were always enough bona fide singers to produce a really good sound – Geoffrey made sure of that.

My two other pantomimes at the Players' were *Babes in the Wood* and *King Charming – or the Blue Bird of Paradise*. In the former I had a really good part as Miss Jones, Governess to the two extremely naughty 'babes' (Sheila Bernette and Josephine Gordon). The whole show had a Scottish flavour, and Joan Sterndale Bennett in the role of 'Lady Beth Macassar (the Babes' Aunty Macassar)' did a wonderful send-up of Lady Macbeth, which included a bizarre sleepwalking scene. We were all dressed in colourful tartans, and as usual the production looked magnificent. I did not enjoy *King Charming* very much. My part of the Wicked Fairy Soussio required me to do a number crouching over an evil cauldron which belched forth obnoxious smoke. I know that stage smoke is supposed to be harmless, but as one who has only missed two shows in nearly forty years, I feel qualified to say that the particular smoke used in that scene must have been an exception to the rule, for I grew hoarser and hoarser as the run continued. I suppose a croaky witch might be vaguely acceptable, but I had quite a lot to sing, and the whole show became rather uncomfortable.

In addition to these three pantomimes, I did several 'Late Joys' (as the music hall bill was known). This origin of this title is interesting; there was a hotel in King Street, Covent Garden, famous for its supper rooms and entertainment, (F.C. Burnand mentions it in his play, *The Colonel*, 1881), at one time owned by W.C. Evans, who had acquired it from its former proprietor, by the name of Joy. So it became 'Evans – late Joy's', eventually ending up, after many vicissitudes, as the Players' Theatre and Supper Rooms. So the name 'Late Joys' (losing the apostrophe) became the title for the Music Hall bill. Appearing in the bill was great fun, calling for timing, eye contact with the audience, and even answering any repartee that might come your way. But there always seemed to be great appreciation for any straight numbers; one or two were usually included. I haven't so far mentioned the dressing room accommodation – if you have ever attempted to put on a Victorian costume in a telephone kiosk, you will have some idea of the space that was available! It was much easier for the Joys, as there were only about eight people involved, but during the pantomime you can imagine the backstage pandemonium! It always amazed me that such beautifully made-up and immaculately dressed artists could emerge, calm, and ready on time, from this chaos!

My next contract was for a tour of *Salad Days*. I had always had an affection for the show since I saw it in the West End in 1955, immediately prior to leaving for the States on the D'Oyly Carte American tour, and I quite fancied the idea of appearing in it. It's a small cast affair – there were just a dozen of us, each playing several parts, necessitating very quick changes – but I was used to that now. I turned up for the first rehearsal to find John Inman and Barry Howard in the cast; they were wonderful in all their roles – particularly as PC Boot and the Police Inspector respectively. John's timing was brilliant; in those early days he had not yet made a name for himself, but I could see even then that he was destined to do so before long. I was to play Mrs Dawes, mother of Timothy, the juvenile lead (only he was not all that juvenile!); Heloise, a beautician; Asphinxia – a dreadful singer in the Cleopatra nightclub, and various other improbable characters.

We were extremely fortunate to have the composer, Julian Slade, at one of the pianos, so the musical side of the show was in excellent hands. He was absolutely delightful to work with. The whole thing was very light-hearted, but, oh – what a lot of dancing! Everyone set to work with great determination, for as usual there was limited rehearsal time. They were a talented lot – with one unhappy exception. There was one member of the cast who couldn't cope with what she had to do, and the roles she had been given were quite important. I had what should have been a very amusing duet with her, but she could neither remember her words nor keep to her vocal line, so what should have been an enjoyable number became a bit of a nightmare. Poor girl – I really don't know how the management came to give her

Valerie Masterson as 'Marguerite' in Faust (Royal Opera House).
Photograph by Andrew March.

Cyril Fletcher's 'Masquerade' at the Pavilion, Sandown 1957.

Principal Boy in 'Dick Whittington' at the Palace Theatre, Westcliff 1958.

'Land of Smiles' with Charles Craig as Sou-Chong (Coliseum).

Andrea Chenier (Sadler's Wells) as the Countess de Coigny, with other cast members.

Bound for Mount Olympus: from L to R Kevin Miller, CM, Leigh Maurice.
Sadler's Wells 'Orpheus in the Underworld'.

'La Vie Parisienne' (Sadler's Wells) CM, Eric Shilling, John Fryatt.

lencienne in Sadler's Wells 'Merry Widow', Auckland, N.Z.

With Miles Gloriosus in 'A Funny Thing Happened on the Way to the Forum', Phoenix, Leicester.

'My Fair Lady', Connaught Theatre, Worthing. Professor Higgins (Thomas Round), Mrs Pearce (CM).

The cast of 'Babes in the Wood' (Players' Theatre).

The cast of 'Salad Days' with John Inman as PC Boot (CM far left).

'Cabaret' - Fräulein Schneider and Herr Schultz (Brian Hewlett), Belgrade Theatre, Coventry.

'Gigi' - Connaught Theatre, Worthing. As Mamita, with Natalie Caron (Gigi).

On tour in Canada with 'Robert and Elizabeth'. Lucy Fenwick and Michael Denison.

Wilson in 'Robert and Elizabeth' Canada 1977.

Sweeney Todd 'the Beggar Woman'.
The Drum, Plymouth.

Mrs. Brown in 'Me and My Girl' Adelphi Thea

the job; she just wasn't up to it. I don't think any of us realised that she was painfully aware of her inadequacy, and consequently very depressed, till tragedy struck while we were playing Great Yarmouth. We arrived at the theatre one morning to collect our mail, and found the police there. Apparently the poor creature had committed suicide during the night by putting her head in the gas oven in her bedsit. We were shocked beyond measure; we had simply not been aware of her state of mind, or naturally we should have tried to help. I feel that a certain amount of blame lay with the management; it was obvious from the start that the girl was not competent, and they should have released her from her contract at the beginning of rehearsals. But as we all know, the show must go on, and a replacement arrived that same afternoon. She was a seasoned performer who had been in *Salad Days* before, and knew exactly what she was doing. We spent the rest of that sad day rehearsing her into the show, which helped to take our minds off things. But you can imagine the atmosphere in the theatre that night; instead of the usual laughter and noise backstage, the dressing rooms were quiet, and everyone spoke in low voices. On stage we smiled and sang and danced as usual, but with very heavy hearts.

Our contracts came to an end after a few more weeks, then it was announced that the tour had been extended. I had the option of staying on, but decided not to do so – in any case I was shortly to get married and decided a little time off would not come amiss! It was then June, 1964, and I thought it would be soon enough if I started to think about work by the end of the summer.

As things turned out, however, I began rehearsals in August for a new musical. Wendy Toye was to direct *Robert and Elizabeth*, (though it began life as *The Barretts and Mr Browning*, which was too cumbersome a title). Sandy Faris would be the musical director, and Malcolm Pride the designer, so it was the *Orpheus* team all over again, especially as June Bronhill had been cast as Elizabeth Barrett. There was not much for me to do – I would dearly have loved to play Wilson, Elizabeth's maid, but Stella Moray had already been chosen for this – and very good she was, too. So I had to settle for a couple of small parts and the understudy to Wilson, but I didn't mind that – I was back among friends, and even more delighted when Gordon Wilcock, who had been in Orpheus in Australia turned up to play Henry Bevan – Cousin Bella's (Sarah Badel) fiance. David Kelsey, an old friend from the Players' was to be Macready in the theatre scene in which I was involved as Mrs Butler, a rather flamboyant actress.

We all loved the show from the start; the score by Ron Grainer was fresh and tuneful, with many suitably operatic moments for June, and some impressive ensembles. Of course, working with Wendy again was wonderful, and those who had not had that pleasure before were soon captivated. The Grand, Leeds, was our first date on the pre-West End tour, and at the end of the dress rehearsal the uppermost thought in everyone's mind was, 'Isn't it *long*?' And it was – nearly four hours. Meetings and consultations went on endlessly, numbers were cut, dialogue pruned, and gradually, by the time we reached the end of our four weeks in Manchester – our next and last out-of-town date, the show, with its new title *Robert and Elizabeth* was ready for the West End.

The intimidating Mr Barrett was played magnificently by John Clements; originally he had been given a song during the intimate scene with Elizabeth when he makes his regular evening visit to her room. He played the rather tense scene impeccably – as one would have expected – but when he came to the song there was one big drawback – he could not sing. As he attempted to do so, the whole stature of his awesome character crumbled. So, wisely, the powers that be decided the song must go, and the scene was much stronger for its omission. Keith Michell was everything one could wish for in a stage Browning – debonair, dashing, positive – and with a very pleasant singing voice. Angela Richards (Henrietta) and Jeremy Lloyd (Captain Surtees Cook) were both funny and sad in their difficult love affair. The whole cast were excellent, and we hoped for a big success and a long run.

A lot of rumours abounded regarding the West End transfer. It seems that the show was intended for Her Majesty's Theatre, but some managerial mishap occurred, resulting in *Robert and Elizabeth* going into the much smaller Lyric. Malcolm Pride's lovely scenery had to be re-constructed to fit, and with such an expensive show the capacity of the theatre was not large enough to make a profit. In spite of this it ran from October 1964 till February 1967 – a total of 948 performances.

We settled in at the Lyric, making ourselves at home in our dressing rooms, anticipating a long run. I shared a room with Stella Moray and Barbara Leigh, which seemed at first a very pleasant arrangement. However, a difference of opinion made life rather difficult: Stella wanted the window open, and Barbara wanted it closed; as for me, well, I couldn't have cared less if it was bricked up, so long as I had some peace! Every time Stella came off stage and found the window closed, she would throw it open with an exclamation of annoyance; when Barbara came into the room she would slam it shut – and so it went on. Apart from that, we got on quite well!

Having settled down to what looked like being a long run, a message came for me from Sadler's Wells, via Wendy. *Orpheus in the Underworld* was to be revived. As had happened with *The Merry Widow* the whole production had been sold to Garnet Carroll in Australia, so everything, from sets to the smallest props must be re-created from scratch. And I was asked to play Calliope again. 'But I'm in *Robert and Elizabeth* now,' I said, 'We've only just opened!' Of course, as both shows were Wendy Toye productions, getting me out of my contract and back to the Wells was a simple matter, especially as the parts I was playing were small and fairly easy to re-cast. Moreover, there was another tempting prospect on the horizon – a European tour in May 1965 which would include *Iolanthe*, and I was invited to do this as well. So I capitulated.

The revival of *Orpheus* set out to be a faithful copy of the old production, which had been such a success, but I couldn't help feeling that much of the subtlety had gone from the costume designs. Everything seemed to be just that bit brighter, larger, and more brash. But only the few of us who had been in the show from the very beginning, and had played it so many times would have noticed, I suppose. The audience certainly found no fault with it, and full houses were once more the order of the day. It seemed to be a fact that whenever the Wells needed some money, *Orpheus* would return to the repertoire. I was certainly called back on a guest contract time and time again for the show during the next few years.

The European tour set out on May 20th; I appeared as Leila in Amsterdam, Prague, Vienna, Frankfurt, Munich and Berlin. The language did not seem to pose the problems I had envisaged, for many laughs came in the expected places, though we had to be ready to cover if they did not. An example of that was in Berlin, after 'When Britain really ruled the waves', when there was an embarrassing silence. I think it was probably too soon after the war to remind the Germans of that fact!

9.

It's time, I think, to depart from the chronological order to which I have adhered so far, and to deal with things in categories instead. West End musicals seem a good thing to start with. *House of Cards*, my first, I have already mentioned, also *Robert and Elizabeth*, but I shall have to return to that, for I was involved in a quite different production at a much later date. Auditioning for anything in the West End is a highly competitive affair; everyone wants the stability of a long run and the prospect of being firmly established in one place – nobody wants to tour any more. I can't say I blame them, but I must admit that I feel rather cross when I hear young actors saying, 'Oh, I don't want to *tour*!' for that is how so many of us learned our trade.

One of the shows in which I spent a year was *Fiddler on the Roof* at Her Majesty's Theatre. They were auditioning for replacements (it had already enjoyed a good run, and showed no sign of coming off) and I was offered the small part of Shandel, mother of Motel the tailor, one of the young leads. I accepted the contract before I had even seen the show, and that night I went to see the performance. Oh dear, I thought – it's so *drab*. I know it's a wonderful musical, but you must remember I was fresh from *Orpheus* and *La Vie Parisienne*, with all the colour and gaiety and fun of operetta, and a greater contrast was impossible to imagine. I tried on my costume in the wardrobe, and sighed. A dull, shabby blouse, a dreary skirt, a headscarf (babushka) which must cover all my hair; that was my first outfit. There was something 'smarter' for the wedding scene, but just as dismal; for this I had to wear a 'sheitel' – a severe wig which did absolutely nothing for me. I learned that Jewish ladies in 1905 Russia, upon their marriage, had all their hair cut off, wearing a babushka by day, and for the Sabbath and special occasions, a sheitel. There was worse to come – make-up was forbidden; we were supposed to look like poor hungry peasants, and nothing achieves this better than a naked face under strong stage lighting, causing the skin to take on a sickly, transparent look. I gazed into the mirror at my pale uninteresting face, framed in the hard unbecoming wig. Ah, well – I told myself with a shrug of resignation – it's just for a year. *Fiddler* is the only show I have ever been in where I had to take my make-up *off* before going on stage!

There were several new members of the cast who joined at the same time as myself; one was Lex Goudsmit, who was to take over the role of Tevye from Topol. He had already played it with great success in the Amsterdam production, and had a fine bass voice. Hy Hazell was to be his wife, Golde. The Rabbi and his son Mendel (Heinz Bernard and Brian Ralph) were also new to their parts. Another actor, Ted Merwood, joined the company at that time to understudy and play a small role, and became a good friend whom I have been destined to meet again many times in different productions over the years. So although it is usually a little nervewracking to join a show in the middle of a run, there were enough of us to become friends before we had to meet the rest of the company. Thus I was able to avoid that exposed feeling at the first rehearsal when you think everyone is watching you. After all, with a new Tevye, who would want to look at *me*?

Looking back on that year, there was much to enjoy. I shared a dressing room with Mia Nardi, who played Chava, the young daughter who causes her family so much grief by marrying out of the Jewish faith. She was from Hungary, and married to Peter Sasdy, director of many of the Hammer horror films. We became friends, and I was sorry when at the end of six months her contract came to an end and I had a new room mate. It turned out that I knew her already – she was Lynn Dalby, and had been a member of the *Salad Days* cast, so we had plenty to talk about. Lynn didn't last long – I never really knew why – maybe the management thought she was unsuitable. If that were the case, I think they should have found it out at the audition; however, she went on to appear opposite Adam Faith in the *Budgie* series, so things obviously turned out well for her. The third Chava was Tina Martin, who had a terrific sense of humour, which suited me very well, and helped the remaining months of my 'sentence' to pass pleasantly. The young Gemma Craven (then Rita Craven) was also a member of the *Fiddler* company at that time, destined for greater things in the years to come.

I liked Hy Hazell enormously. We met once by accident on a bus from Victoria station to the theatre, and chatted about all and sundry during the journey. I asked her about her unusual name, and she told me it was short for 'Hyacinth Primrose' with which she had apparently been lumbered by rather thoughtless parents! As we made our exit together at one point in the show, when we both had a fairly long break, she would often invite me to her room for a crafty gin and tonic. I had the impression that her private life was not altogether happy; she confided a little to me, and I listened and sympathised. Sometimes her singing on stage betrayed her distress of mind, particularly during 'Sunrise, sunset'; I stood near her in that scene, and could tell when she was feeling particularly emotional – maybe the nostalgic nature of that number did not help. One evening we came into the theatre for the performance to find the atmosphere unusually quiet. We were told that Hy had died the previous night after the show, having choked during a meal. It was all very strange. I had had a drink with her during the previous night's performance, and she had seemed rather upset then, but I just chatted as usual and tried to cheer her up a little. I had grown fond of her, and was very upset by the tragic events. Poor Anna Tzelniker, who had been playing Yente the Matchmaker, had to go on as Golde at that performance. She did not use Hy's dressing room – she could not bear to, and we were a very subdued company that night.

I grew quite fond of *Fiddler* during that year, and intrigued to learn about Jewish customs and religious practices. I found the Sabbath scene particularly moving, and the whole show more interesting as I became accustomed to it. Most importantly, the houses were always packed and the reception tremendous at the final curtain. When Lex Goudsmit's contract ended, Alfie Bass came in to play Tevye, and brought a new dimension to the role. The continuing capacity audiences were a big boost to the morale, a feature which did not apply to another musical in which I spent nearly a year – *Gone With the Wind* at Drury Lane. Never heard of it? I am not surprised. Although I was in it for so long I cannot remember a single tune from the show! Whoever thought that such a long epic tale could be turned into a musical had made a great mistake – it couldn't. They seem to have managed it with *Les Miserables*, which, although not my cup of tea, has certainly been successful. *Gone With the Wind*, however, was a failure. Ten months of course is not a disgraceful run, but the production was nursed along, the house was generously 'papered' (*we* never got any complimentary tickets) and the matinee audiences were painfully thin. We heard that it was destined for the USA, but the Americans would only be interested if it achieved a decent run in London first. So in my opinion it was kept going for far too long, for the purpose of maintaining their interest, which in the end it failed to do.

Auditions were beyond belief. I was recalled five times before being offered the minute part of Mrs Meade, the doctor's wife. Competition was fierce, for who would not want to be in a big new prestigious musical at Drury Lane? Joe Layton, a well-known American director was in charge of the production, with Ray Cook as musical director. June Ritchie was cast in the demanding role of Scarlett, with Harve Presnell as Rhett Butler, Robert Swann as Ashley Wilkes, and Patricia Michaels as Melanie Hamilton. Two ex-D'Oyly Carters besides myself were among the cast: Mercia Glossop, and Harry Goodier, who played Scarlett's father, Gerald O'Hara. He had a nice solo at the beginning of the show, which showed off his fine baritone voice – and his D'Oyly Carte diction. The cast was enormous, with many extras in addition to the actors, and whatever I may have to say about the show, the sets and costumes were magnificent. The technical effects were unbelievable – Atlanta burned and collapsed before our eyes, and you can imagine how much rehearsal that scene needed to prevent any genuine fatalities. The poor horse, Charlie, had to stand there throughout all the noise and tumult, which he did stoically, bless his heart. He was carefully fed and watered at a regular time so that he would not blot his copybook by doing what comes naturally while on stage, but the owners had not taken into consideration the fact that the first night started at 7pm, and not 7.30! So dear old Charlie, with perfect timing, deposited a neat pile in the middle of the stage at a particularly dramatic moment! He received equal billing with the two stars in the press next day.

Rehearsals went on for ever, and we were kept in the theatre all the hours that Equity would permit. Music calls in the dress circle bar would occupy us every moment that we were not needed on stage, with costume fittings squeezed in somehow. I remember my opening crinoline in blue-grey organza, with cuffs and collar trimmed with the finest lace which I'm sure could not even be seen by the conductor, never mind the audience. I was told that this dress cost £500 – (I don't suppose that figure included the bonnet, shoes, wig etc) and that was in 1972! I wore it for ten minutes at the most. I never cease to marvel at the unnecessary expense involved in stage costumes; what is the use of fine expensive trimmings which cannot be seen from the front? Nobody enjoys wearing opulent costumes more than I, but wonderful effects can be achieved by using far less costly materials. The mind boggles at the thought of the total bill for dressing *Gone With the Wind*; a long run would have helped recoup the outlay for the producer, Harold Fielding, but unfortunately that did not happen. I made some good friends during those ten months, and we commiserated with one another about the tedious nature of the show, and the constant rehearsals. We all had a quick change before the finale; Bill Drysdale, one of the dancers, and I found a convenient little spot in the wings where we set our final costumes in advance. Much gossip was exchanged during those few hectic moments, as we leapt out of one costume and into another – wild rumours such as 'I've heard the notice is going up on Saturday!' or 'we're only running till the end of the month!' All just wishful thinking.

There was a dreary number for the whole company, sung at Scarlett's daughter Bonnie's funeral, 'Bonnie gone', which we would rehearse several times a week, often coming in early to do so. It was a fairly complicated ensemble, but it really didn't warrant all that attention, for no amount of vocal excellence could have made it remotely interesting. A word about Bonnie here; as is the rule with under-age actors, there were three little girls alternating in the role, one of whom was Bonnie Langford. She was by far the best of the three, and a real little pro, getting on with the job in a most business-like manner. I have followed her subsequent career with great interest, and on the rare occasions when we have happened to meet, we've always had a laugh about *Gone With the Wind* – at one point in the show she was escorted on stage by a couple of ladies, of whom I was one.

I understudied Aunt Pitty-Pat, who was played by Bessie Love, an old film star. She was such a dear, though I shouldn't imagine anyone in the audience could hear a word she was saying. I never had a chance to go on for her – that didn't bother me, but it meant even more rehearsals. It did seem at times that we were never out of that theatre.

A few years later I auditioned for another musical, which was vastly different, and much more to my taste. *My Fair Lady* had been running at the Adelphi with great success, and contracts for some of the company were coming to an end, so replacements were needed. There was an illustrious cast: Tony Britton as Professor Higgins, Anna Neagle as his mother, and Peter Bayliss as Doolittle. Robin Midgley had originally directed the show, which had begun its successful career at the Haymarket, Leicester. Gillian Lynne was responsible for the choreography and musical staging, Tim Goodchild designed the costumes, Adrian Vaux the sets, and the musical director was Anthony Howard Williams, (popularly known as Anthony Handbag Williams, for reasons that I was never able to determine). Liz Robertson, who had received such acclaim as Eliza, was soon to marry Alan J Lerner, and to be replaced by Jill Martin. I knew Jill from *Fiddler*, in which she had played the second daughter, Hodel. The small roles allotted to me were Mrs Hopkins, a rumbustious Cockney lady who has an altercation with Doolittle, Lady Boxington in the Ascot scene, and in Act II the Queen of Transylvania. I was also to understudy Dame Anna Neagle, and, as it turned out, to play Mrs Higgins many times. I had plenty of individual rehearsal with the dance captain before being put into the show, and was glad of it; the highly-stylised Ascot scene requires perfect synchronisation to be really effective, and I would have hated to turn left when everyone else turned right! As usual, people were very friendly and helpful, and I was soon at ease in what proved to be a very enjoyable show.

Those of us who can remember Cecil Beaton's famous black and white Ascot scene in the original production at Drury

Lane will find it hard to imagine any other setting, but Tim Goodchild created a most attractive scene in apple green and pink, with many frills and furbelows, and the most enormous hats. My role in this – Lady Boxington – was almost nothing, but ensured me a good seat near the front, and plenty of acting opportunities!

I shared a large dressing room with four other girls, and once I was familiar with the show, we got up to all sorts of things. Someone had a recipe for 'bread champagne', which seemed amazingly simple; all you had to do was to spread some yeast on slices of toast and leave it to soak in a gallon of water for about a week, then strain and bottle it, and leave it to mature for a few weeks. Shirley Greenwood brought in a toaster, and we set about toasting the best part of a sliced loaf; the smell of burning bread permeated the theatre, causing consternation backstage. 'Where's the fire?' shouted someone, and we hastily pushed the toaster into a cupboard and opened a window, poking our heads round the dressing room door with expressions of innocence. We eventually managed to put all the ingredients into a plastic bucket, covered it and concealed it carefully where we hoped nobody would look. We took turns to stir it every day; great was the anticipation of a constant supply of cheap champagne, and we informed the other dressing rooms that we were making it (we did not reveal the recipe!) and would shortly be dispensing our wonderful concoction. Enquiries came daily about its progress, and we answered enthusiastically that it would not be long. The truth is, the contents of the bucket looked daily more sinister; green layers of mould started to form on the surface – could that be right? Finally a stagnant smell began to emanate from the cupboard where the 'champagne' was kept, and we were forced to conclude that the project was a failure. But we were determined not to admit this to the others, so what to do? We decided to manufacture a credible drink from some cheap sparkling wine, cider, and a little lager; this we mixed carefully, and invited all to taste, only allowing each person a tiny amount. 'It's quite nice,' was the general opinion – how we laughed! But I still wonder where we went wrong.

Soon after joining *My Fair Lady* I found I had to go on for Mrs Higgins while Dame Anna took a week's holiday. I was well rehearsed, and quite looked forward to it. On the Saturday night before this, Anna came to me in the wings. 'Now, dear, I hope you're going to use my dressing room,' she said. 'You'll find glasses in the top cupboard, tea and coffee below, and – oh, there's a bottle of wine in the fridge!' What a delightful person Anna was – not a bit 'starry', even after the fantastic career she'd had. And when I went into the dressing room on the Monday night there was a big bowl of flowers on the table, with a card: 'Have a wonderful week – Anna'.

I loved playing Mrs Higgins, and Tony Britton was a delight to work with. I particularly enjoyed the conservatory scene, and was gratified to get the usual laugh on her exit line. I was not sure if I would, that first night; it is always a little disappointing for an audience to arrive at the theatre and find that a big star like Anna Neagle will not be appearing. However, they seemed not to mind too much, and applause and laughter came where they should.

As the weeks went on, more contracts came up for renewal, and one or two more people left. One was Betty Paul, who had been playing Mrs Pearce; the current Mrs Eynsford Hill (Joan Ryan) stepped up into her place, and I was promoted to Joan's old role, moving in to share a room with her – (I would miss my lively companions!) I had a much easier time in my new part, no longer having to be in the big scene, 'I'm getting married in the morning' which went on for ever, but sitting with my feet up instead.

The end of the London run arrived, but it was not to be the end of the show. There was to be a short tour, then the whole production would be going over to Toronto for a six week season at the Royal Alexandra Theatre. Many of the cast left when we finished at the Adelphi, so when the company assembled at a hall in Chiswick to rehearse for Canada, under the eagle eye of Gillian Lynne, there were quite a number of new faces. My new 'son', Freddy, was now to be played by Peter Fleetwood instead of Michael Sadler; we soon established a splendid mother and son relationship – so splendid, in fact, that he has sent me a Mother's Day card ever since! Rebecca Caine was the new Eliza; Anna Neagle, Tony Britton and Richard Caldicot (Colonel Pickering) were to continue in their usual roles. It would be my third visit to Canada.

I was fortunate in having a very good friend in Toronto, with whom I had worked in Chichester, some years previously. Michael Burgess had since become a priest in the Church of England; as well as his full time post as chaplain to a boys' school, he was at that time assisting the Rector of St Anne's, his friend Warren Eling. Both assured me there was plenty of room at the Rectory, so I accepted their invitation to stay, and spent an extremely happy time there. One weekend Anna invited one of the dancers, Robert Moore, and myself to go on a trip to Niagara Falls; her companion, Joyce Wright (not *that* one!) had hired a car, and would drive us there and back, returning by way of Niagara-on-the-Lake. We had such a pleasant day; I had been to the Falls years before while on the D'Oyly Carte tour, but was only too keen to see them again. Anna played every performance in Toronto, so I was not called upon to deputise for her. She looked so very frail, but there was a wiriness and sense of purpose about her which kept her going – and of course that sheer professionalism which made her determined not to disappoint her audience. She was one of the nicest people I ever met in the theatre world.

10.

Still on the subject of the big West End musical, we come now to another of my favourites – *Me and My Girl*. First put on in 1937 at the Victoria Palace, it was revised and re-written, the new production opening at the end of 1984 at the Haymarket Theatre, Leicester, from where so many musicals made successful transfers to the West End. As with any such show, people fell over one another to get into it, and the auditions (appropriately at the Victoria Palace) were inundated with hopefuls. Most of us had appointments made for us by our agents, but there were so many candidates that there was a lot of waiting about involved. However, the management was very considerate, and unlike *Gone With the Wind*, we were not called back again and again, but after auditioning were told at once if we would be required for a re-call, which would be later that day. Finally, only very few of us were left, then, oh dear – we were set a dance routine to do. Now, I can cope with most of the dancing required in musicals, but I must have time to take it in and work it out. The steps that were set were (to me) rather complicated, but I was fortunate indeed, for the choreographer was Gillian Gregory, with whom I had recently worked in the musical, *Cabaret*, at the Belgrade, Coventry. 'Oh, I know *you* can do it,' she said to me, 'Go and sit down!' Lucky me – I was accepted, and given the small part of Lady Brighton, plus the understudy to the Duchess of Dene, which I later played many times.

When the *Me and My Girl* company assembled in the rehearsal room in Leicester, I looked curiously round at the cast. Robert Lindsay was to play Bill Snibson, the Cockney

lad who turned out to be the heir to a peerage, Frank
Thornton, famous for his role of Captain Peacock in *Are
You Being Served*, was cast as Sir John, Ursula Smith the
Duchess, Susannah Fellows her daughter Jacqueline,
Richard Caldicot, Charles, the butler – and who was the
rather eccentrically dressed girl with the punk hair-do?
Which role could she be playing? She was, it turned out,
Emma Thompson, and she was going to play opposite Bob
Lindsay as Sally Smith.

We worked long and hard on the show, but there was a good
feeling about it from the start. I remember the first complete
run-through with the orchestra; it was a wet and gloomy
evening, and we were in a most depressing church hall.
Dripping raincoats hung from hooks and chairs, wellies
littered the floor, dancers' clothes were strewn about – you
could not imagine a more uninspiring venue. But as soon as
the music started, an air of excitement permeated that dismal
place, and grew as the rehearsal proceeded; nobody chatted
or made any noise – we were somehow caught up in the
most magical atmosphere, and knew then and there that
the show would be a success, though nobody at that point
could have envisaged the eight-year run that it achieved.

Rehearsals were, on the whole, enjoyable affairs – that is,
until I met my Waterloo at the beginning of the second act.
The number was 'The Sun Has Got His Hat On', sung by
Gerald (Jacqueline's would-be fiancé, played by Robert
Longden) and we had to tap dance! The dancers did the
most complicated part of the routine, but all the other
characters had to join in. I was surprised at the number of
people who were proficient in this particular skill – the most

unlikely folk turned up with tap shoes, and there they were – tapping away like mad. I went right to the back while the routine was being set, and felt quite desperate – would I ever manage it, I wondered. But I persevered, buttonholed Anita Pashley, (who was playing a small role and understudying Emma Thompson and Susannah Fellows) to give me a bit of coaching whenever possible, and gradually I achieved some semblance of tap dancing. I was immensely relieved, for I loved the show, and that had so far been the only fly in the ointment.

The period was the thirties, so the costumes were elegant and comfortable to wear; I got away without a wig, as my hair was suitably short. This made life much easier, though I normally prefer to wear a wig on stage. It gives you something substantial to anchor hats and head-dresses to, but in this case there was no problem – thirties hats being very easy to manage. The opening scene, when we were a group of socialites on our way to a 'Weekend in Hareford' (Bill's ancestral home to be) by gracious invitation of the Duchess, was ingenious. We were bowling along in what looked like a large open sports car, but as we got out at the end of the number, each person took a suitcase, which was actually part of the vehicle. When we were all out with our luggage, the car had vanished – the effect was remarkable. The sets (by Martin Johns) were tremendously effective; the splendour of Hareford Hall, peopled by a crowd of wealthy guests, dissolved effortlessly into the kitchen scene, with full retinue of uniformed staff by means of revolves. The drawing room, the library, the Hareford Arms and a street scene in Lambeth materialised similarly. But surely the most striking scene of all was when the Hareford ancestors descended from their picture frames – now, what does *that* remind me of? Yes, of course – a direct crib from *Ruddigore* – only the Hareford chaps did a smart tap routine before returning to their frames! (G & S producers, please note!) With regard to the cast, Robert Lindsay was superb as Bill – his comedy, timing, and his endearing characterisation were perfect. His opposite number, Emma Thompson, was at first rather a puzzle. One would not have immediately cast her as Sally, though there was undoubtedly enormous talent there. She worked extremely hard at the role, and there was great sincerity in her portrayal; her rendering of the sad little ballad 'When You Lose Your Heart' was intensely moving. I grew to like Emma very much; she would occasionally get into the same carriage of the Bakerloo line train I was travelling on at West Hampstead on the way to the theatre, and we chatted all the way to Charing Cross. She always seemed interested to hear what other people were doing rather than talk about herself. I have followed her career with great interest and admiration, and on the few occasions I have sent a card to congratulate her on some success or other, she has never failed to reply.

The press notices for *Me and My Girl* were excellent, both in Leicester – and, more importantly, in London. In one paper, everyone in the cast received the highest praise – with the exception of Emma. Her notice simply said, 'Sally was played by Emma Thompson – a large girl in a print frock'. Most young actresses starting out on their career would have been devastated; not Emma, or at least, she didn't show it. From then on, when she had occasion to send a note to anyone, she would sign it: 'from Large Girl in Print Frock'!

As the show settled down I went on for the Duchess many times, occasionally for reason of illness, but also, in a long run everyone has to have a holiday, and Ursula Smith, who became a good friend, was no exception. I really did enjoy it, and loved working with Frank Thornton. The Duchess and Sir John originally had a duet near the end of the show, which was later cut – I can't imagine why; it explained the old love affair between the two of them, and was both funny and charming. I often sing it at concerts with John Fryatt, and it always goes well. I can only assume that the director, Mike Ockrent, felt that, coming so near the end, it held up the pace of the show. It didn't feel like that, and seemed to be greatly appreciated by the audience, providing a few moments of quiet amusement before the jollity of the finale.

Eventually Bob's and Emma's contracts came to an end, and their roles were re-cast. Enn Reitel, whom I did not know, came in to play Bill. To my mind he lacked Bob's impudent charm and quicksilver humour, but the show went bubbling on as usual. The new Sally was none other than Su Pollard – a rather surprising choice, but much loved by the audience. I had by then been promoted to the role of Mrs Brown, Sally's landlady, and we had a bit together in the Lambeth scene in Act II, which involved a lot of looking out of windows and running in and out of doors. How we laughed (not on stage, of course!) – Su is just as funny off stage as on – she's a natural comedienne. She is also a very kind and considerate person; not a day went by without her visiting all the dressing rooms before the show to see how everyone was. Talking of dressing rooms, I was put in a large one with four other small part people; this was fine, and on the second floor – quite good for the Adelphi, which has hundreds of stairs. Anita

Pashley, who was understudying the two leading female roles, found herself in a room with all the rest of the girls. She was not at all pleased with this, as she felt she needed a bit of peace and quiet to listen to the tannoy and learn the roles as quickly as possible. She explored the theatre, going right to the top of the building, and found an empty room, which she decided would be just the thing. Visiting her there, I remarked how nice and peaceful it was, and she asked me to join her. No sooner said than done; the lace curtains went up, the window boxes went out, and there we were, comfortably ensconced in the Penthouse Suite. Although we were right at the top, up many stairs if you couldn't get the lift – which was usually the case – our room seemed to be where everything happened.

We produced a dreadful company magazine, 'The Dressing Room Mirror' to which everyone contributed, Anita typing away busily every time she had a few minutes off stage. When you're in a long run it's most important to have plenty of backstage activities, and a good party every now and then to keep up the company morale. We decided to hold a weekly raffle, with a small but interesting prize; a percentage of the proceeds would go to a chosen charity, and the rest to a party fund. It was called the 'Round the World' raffle, and a different country was chosen each week, the nature of the prize being dictated by the land in question. I liased with Su over this – she was an enthusiastic participant, and I was the one who shopped for the prizes. I remember buying a delicate china cup and saucer and a packet of Lapsang Souchong when China was selected as the country of the week! When sufficient money had been collected, a company party was held, and we began fund raising again, with a new idea to tempt people to join in. At Christmas we had a decorated dressing room competition; this we had to do with great care, and consultation with the fireman. Anita and I decided to make a model of Hareford Hall and the surrounding village in one corner of the room – no mean feat! She was so clever with the cutting out and assembling of the buildings, which were made of cornflake packets, tissue boxes – any cardboard we could lay hands on – while I did all the painting. The church was the piece de resistance; we made 'stained glass' windows from which light streamed out over the polystyrene snow, together with the sound of a choir singing 'Silent Night' by means of a miniature tape recorder cunningly concealed within. Nobody was allowed in while this masterpiece was being constructed; Bob and Emma were specially invited to the opening ceremony, at which they received a glass of wine. After that, the Penthouse Suite was the focus of attention as everyone flocked to see this amazing work of art!

And so the weeks and months rolled by. At last, after fifteen months at the Adelphi, in addition to the Leicester season, I felt I'd had enough and it was time to go. I had a chance to go to Cardiff to do an important role in a musical at the Sherman Theatre, (more of that anon) so that helped me to make up my mind. I'd made many friends in *Me and My Girl*, one in particular – David Alder, with whom I'd had such a laugh during the show. We've kept in touch ever since, and I was pleased to see him in *She Loves Me* at the Savoy, in which he was such a success some years later.

My next two West End musicals were less to my liking, and I did not spend long in either of them. The first was *Can-Can* at the Strand Theatre, preceded by a season at the Alhambra, Bradford, and the second *Anything Goes* at the Prince Edward, both by Cole Porter. *Can-Can* seemed to be a doubtful starter from the very beginning. It was certainly not the fault of the cast; it starred Milo O'Shea (an Irish charmer playing a Frenchman!) and Donna McKechnie, the American actress who had made such a mark in *A Chorus Line* at Drury Lane. I had a very strange character to play – Madame Legrand – a sinister figure dressed completely in black, with a heavy veil, who owned various doubtful establishments in Montmartre. The show had been re-vamped, with some original numbers taken out and others put in. The dialogue during rehearsals was hardly ever the same two days running, with cuts and re-writes constantly being given to us. The same thing went on even after the show had opened; I remember being handed a new piece of dialogue before the performance one day that had to go in that evening. There was a short rehearsal before the half-hour, and that was all. At the Strand all sorts of mishaps occurred – several times the tabs stuck, and we were sent home after the interval – I felt that the whole production was a chapter of accidents from beginning to end. What a pity – the cast were all such a friendly lot, and two old chums – Norman Warwick, of Players' Theatre fame, and Peter Durkin from *Gone With the Wind* were in the company. The run – not unexpectedly – was quite short.

The other musical, *Anything Goes*, was another matter. It had already had a good innings, and the time had come to re-cast. Elaine Page's role of Reno was taken over – wonderfully, I thought, by Louise Gold, but somehow the audiences didn't like the changes and stopped coming in sufficient numbers. Rather a pity, for I had not been in it long, and although I had a tiny role, I was understudy to Mrs Harcourt (played by my old friend Ursula Smith) and went on for that part a number of times. I had a small dressing room to myself, which made life very pleasant, and my Penthouse Suite companion, Anita Pashley, was also in the cast.

Musicals put on by repertory companies, though usually produced on a shoestring, can often be of a very high standard. Rehearsal time is comparatively short, and the number of performances limited, so nobody has time to become bored. In fact, just as you are really beginning to relax and enjoy yourself, you find it is the last night! I did several shows at the Connaught Theatre, Worthing, one of which springs to mind because of its G & S associations. It was *My Fair Lady*, with which I was very familiar, only this time I was to play Mrs Pearce, Professor Higgins's landlady. Imagine my amazement when I arrived at the theatre for the first rehearsal to find that Higgins was to be played by Tom Round, Doolittle by Donald Adams, and Eliza by Evette Davis! Four ex-Carte singers in one show. We had some fun about that. Tom, contrary to tradition, actually *sang* all the notes that Frederick Loewe had written – nobody had ever heard them before! Don was quite the best Doolittle I have ever seen – his 'Get Me to the Church on Time' number was sensational, and he leapt about the stage like a two-year-old. Evette was a charming and spirited Eliza, and although I had never met her before, that peculiar D'Oyly Carte magic made us feel like old friends. Altogether, I doubt if the Connaught had ever heard such singing. Naturally it was a very modest production compared with the West End one I had been in previously, but with a cast like that it achieved a remarkable standard.

One of my favourite musicals is *Cabaret*, and I have been fortunate to be in it three times – at the Connaught, Worthing, the Everyman, Cheltenham, and the Belgrade, Coventry. They were three very different productions, and I am not sure that I can single out any one as being the best. *Cabaret* is by virtue of its setting a very serious piece of musical theatre; true, it has its amusing moments, and there are many touches of humour, but always with a bitter flavour. When I speak of *Cabaret*, the musical, I advise you to forget the film, which bears little resemblance to the show. The two roles which most clearly show the imminent menace of the Nazi jackboot are those of the ill-fated elderly lovers, Herr Schultz, the Jewish greengrocer, and Fräulein Schneider – these are almost non-existent in the movie. Schultz visits Fräulein Schneider regularly in the rather grim lodging house which she runs, courting her with gifts from his shop in the most delightful, old-fashioned way. Their duet, 'It Couldn't Please Me More', when he presents her with a pineapple is at once charming and sad, and, when finally Fräulein Schneider is forced to give up her gentle suitor on account of his being Jewish, she has an angry, bitter song, reminiscent of Kurt Weill, which she sings to Sally and Cliff, asking 'What would you do?' Playing Schneider was very moving, and I always became deeply immersed in the character, and influenced by the frightening atmosphere of the gathering political storm. I had three wonderful Schultzes – Donald Scott, Kalman Glass, and Brian Hewlett, who plays Neil Carter in *The Archers*, of which I am a great fan. It is nice to hear him regularly in the programme, and his role of Neil could hardly be farther removed from that of Herr Schultz!

Sally Bowles is a complicated character to get right; the three with whom I was concerned were June Shand, Sara Clee, and Eleanor Davies (now David). The latter name may ring a bell with some of you, for she played Mrs Fanny Ronalds in Mike Leigh's excellent film *Topsy-Turvy*. Sally Bowles was one of Eleanor's first big roles in the theatre, and she was quite scared of it. I shared a dressing room with her, and tried to give her confidence, for that was all she needed, and I believe I did help a bit. She and Richard Kates (Cliff) gave me a pair of stone tortoises, which I still have in the garden – they are getting a bit weathered now, like their owner!

Gigi was another success at the Worthing Connaught, and Nick Young, the director, managed to get Natalie Caron, Lesley Caron's niece, for the title role. I played Gigi's grandmother, Mamita, which was great fun, especially the famous 'I Remember it Well' duet with Paul Bacon, who was doing a marvellous Maurice Chevalier re-creation. Wonderful music, all of it, and 'The Night They Invented Champagne' always received a tremendous reception.

I was pleased to work again with John Inman, this time in *A Funny Thing Happened on the Way to the Forum* at the Phoenix Theatre, Leicester. My role was that of Domina, the overbearing wife of old Senex, and John was my slave, Hysterium. Once again his comedy and timing were brilliant, and I fear that without meaning to he eclipsed the leading character Pseudolus (John Bluthal). Larry Drew, who had been in the original cast of *The Boy Friend* at

Wyndham's Theatre, and whom I knew from the Players', choreographed, others in the cast were Michael Sadler (Hero) and Roy Macready (Lycus), both of whom I was to work with again in *My Fair Lady* and *Me and My Girl* respectively. It was a complicated production, with an intricate set full of windows and doors, and there is a frantic chase towards the end of the show, with characters in disguise being hotly pursued by all the wrong people for the wrong reasons. Such a mix-up ensued as we rushed in and out of doors, climbed out of windows and generally got into a terrible muddle. To rehearse this was pure chaos, and took for ever. We were still trying to sort out the comings and goings when the half-hour call came on the first night, and we hadn't got as far as the finale! That, fortunately, was fairly simple, so the show got on somehow, but there were more rehearsals the next day to tidy up. Once running, the whole thing was hilarious, but rather exhausting. I used to give John Inman a lift to London every weekend, and we would race down the M1 after the show on Saturday night in my small Fiat 500, and back on the Monday afternoon – fun while it lasted, but I wasn't terribly sorry when we came to the last performance!

11.

The Wizard of Oz is a show I have been in three times, in three different productions at three different theatres. The first was in Leicester, at the Phoenix, way back in 1969, when I played Aunt Em and the Sorceress of the North. The production was entirely for children – they had even been involved in a competition to design the costumes, which was a very good idea. I had a splendid white witch's outfit covered with a jolly pattern, and a tall pointed hat. The only drawback was that on many days the performances were at 10am and 2pm. The horror of hearing the half-hour called at 9.25am is something I shall leave to your imagination. But all in all it was a happy few weeks, and I made a very good friend during my stay. Our accompanist, Julia Josephs, was – and still is – an extremely accomplished pianist, and we soon discovered that we had many interests in common. We have been close friends ever since.

My second *Wizard of Oz* was many years later – 1983-4, to be precise, at the Churchill Theatre, Bromley. This was a much more sophisticated affair, with a cast of well-known actors. I was to appear again as Aunt Em and the Good Witch; the Wicked Witch of the West was Fenella Fielding, and the Cowardly Lion was Charlie Drake. The show was directed by David Kelsey, whom I knew very well from *Robert and Elizabeth* and the Players'. I had been warned by several people, 'Fenella Fielding – oh, she's a difficult lady,' so I was filled with trepidation at the first rehearsal, for I had several scenes with her. Nothing could have been farther from the truth – we hit it off at once, and she became a good friend. I used to meet her at Notting Hill Gate to drive down to

Bromley, for she was not above travelling in my small Fiat 500 (a newer one!) and we would chat and put the world to rights all the way to the theatre. The costumes were wonderful, and very witty. I looked like a pink puffball in my cloud of tulle, with pink curly wig to match, and plenty of glitter in all the right places. Perhaps it could be said that Fenella was difficult where the wardrobe was concerned, for she refused to wear the dress designed for her, and demanded quite a different outfit. She was absolutely right; the traditional black witch's costume and tall hat did not suit her unique personality in the least. She got what she wanted – a slinky black dress and deep auburn wig – a rather Cruella de Vil sort of thing, which suited her perfectly, looked sinisterly chic, and contrasted with my costume wonderfully well. I looked as if I'd bought mine in C & A, while she'd gone shopping at Harrods! There was an excellent rapport between us, and we still exchange Christmas cards. Of Charlie Drake I know nothing at all; whereas all the rest of the cast were very soon on friendly terms, he only came out of his dressing room to go on stage, otherwise his door remained firmly shut. I sent him a card and a Lion bar on the first night; there was absolutely no response.

I did not enjoy my third *Wizard of Oz* at all. Towards the end of the Bromley season I was approached to do one week in Leeds, at the Grand; the production had been on tour for some time, and the management proposed to extend the run with a week in Leeds. All the cast were free to do this with the exception of Avril Angers, who had been playing the Sorceress of the North, with the result that they contacted my agent to see if I would agree to deputise for her for the final week. I wasn't very keen on the idea, but the very nice fee offered persuaded me to take it on. I had one week free between Bromley and Leeds; the company were at the Congress, Eastbourne during that time, so I went down to see the show. I didn't like it very much. The production was much broader than David Kelsey's; there were ponies and some dreadful 'Waltzing Waters' which probably sent most of the children rushing to the loo. These gushed up across the back of the stage and were illuminated with lurid colours; what they had to do with *The Wizard of Oz* I cannot imagine – or the ponies either, for that matter. The whole thing was really like a pantomime. My costume, though quite pretty, was just a conventional fairy queen type outfit, which did not inspire me much.

Peter Sallis, of *Last of the Summer Wine* fame, was the Lion, Geoffrey Bayldon the Scarecrow, Christophey Beeny the Tin Man, and Tessa Wyatt Dorothy – all well-known television personalities of the time. I soon got the hang of the production, though it was vastly different from the Bromley one. What I found so very strange was the lack of friendliness of the cast. I was of course introduced to them all, but there it ended. I had my own dressing room, but nobody ever came to visit, or to ask how I was getting on, with the result that I felt extremely lonely. I was glad when the last performance was over – I believe I left the theatre without saying goodbye to anyone except my dresser and the stage doorman!

I have always wanted to do more straight acting, but musicals seemed to crop up all the time. I did play an eccentric aunt in Agatha Christie's *Love from a Stranger* at the Connaught, Worthing, but since then had not had the opportunity to do any straight work. I heard that a new Rattigan double bill was to open at the Duchess; the shorter of the two plays was a send-up of the *Tosca* story, and they were looking for a walking understudy for Joan Greenwood, who would also be required to sing a few bits of 'Vissi d'Arte' (*Tosca's* big aria) offstage. I went along to the audition and met the director, the formidable John Dexter, ready to sing whichever part of the aria he chose. 'What key would you like it in?' he asked. I was horrified, and showed it. 'What *key*?' I said scathingly, 'There's only *one* key for 'Vissi d'Arte!' So I sang it in the correct key, read some dialogue, and got the job. If I had known it at the time, I had treated Mr Dexter in exactly the right way, for as rehearsals proceeded, I saw that the few people who stood up to him fared much better than those who quailed before his sarcasm. I had to sit in at all the rehearsals, and watched with concern as he gradually undermined Joan Greenwood's confidence. 'Can't hear you!' he bellowed from the front. She was such a dear, and that was not the way to treat anyone of her calibre, though she never complained. The two plays, *Before Dawn* and *After Lydia* formed the double bill, under the title of *In Praise of Love*; Donald Sinden co-starred with Joan in both plays. I was backstage for the former of course, and sang my pieces of the aria before Joan made her entrance. She was a very sweet person, and most complimentary. On the last night she gave me a little book of poems, and wrote in it: 'To the Beautiful Voice'!

A 'walking understudy' does not go on stage, but must be in the theatre on the half-hour and remain until the person they cover has made his or her last entrance. I occasionally stayed in the dressing room for the entire performance, but more often sat out front for the second play. John Dexter stopped me one day on my way round to the front of house and said, 'Will you tell me if you can *hear* Miss Greenwood?' I'm afraid I replied that I did not think it was my job to do that. To sit out front and report on a fellow artist would have been a most unprofessional thing to do.

The season at the Duchess was a fairly short one, but I read in *The Stage* some months later that *In Praise of Love* was out on tour. Apparently the first piece, the *Tosca* send-up, was no longer part of the content of the evening but the other, formerly *After Lydia*, had been extended to a full-length play. I had always preferred the latter, which, though it has plenty of amusing moments, is actually very moving. To give a brief synopsis – Lydia suffers from leukaemia; she is adamant that her husband Sebastian must not know. In fact, he does know, having discovered some relevant letters, but realising she wants to keep it from him, pretends ignorance. That is a very basic account of the plot – there is humour and heartache, and the two roles are at once amusing and tragic. They are supported by the friend (who does know the truth) and the son (who does not). Donald Sinden was not doing the tour, I read; he had been replaced by John Gregson.

Suddenly the phone rang. Joan Greenwood was ill – there was no understudy – would I be prepared to travel down to the Nuffield Theatre, Southampton, where the company was playing, and go on for Lydia that night? I went hot and cold in turn at the idea. Playing the role even in the original version after months without giving it a thought would be bad enough. But to tackle it in its new extended form would be a nightmare – almost impossible, surely. But if I did not, the play would close. I can say with absolute truth that nobody else in the country knew the part at all; *In Praise of Love* had received its premiere at the Duchess; now it was on tour. It had never been released for performance to any other management, so there was simply nobody to approach in this emergency but me! The revised script was rushed to me, and an hour or so later I was on the train to Southampton, trying to commit to memory as much of the new text as possible. I could not have considered attempting it at all were it not for the fact that the greater part of the play was identical with the original, which I could revise quickly; the added dialogue was another matter.

I arrived at the Nuffield to find the rest of the cast assembled, and waiting for me. There was the great John Gregson, whom I was to play opposite – it seemed like a dream, verging on a nightmare. I had no time at all to dwell upon the mammoth task I was taking on, or to worry about appearing with such a great star – I had to suppress memories of *Genevieve*, and all the fine films I had seen him in, and just get on with the job. Everyone helped and supported me; I had managed to recall the dialogue and moves of the shorter version, and was fairly quickly assimilating the unfamiliar ones, but there was too much to take in all at once. We arranged that I should have odd bits of script and cues hidden round the stage – a Radio Times I could pick up and idly look at, a book I could open and pretend to read. Desperate measures require desperate means – I realised the truth of that at the Nuffield that Monday night. We worked until the half, then I tried on my costumes – it was modern dress of course, so no problems there. When 'beginners' was called I was past caring, and somehow, with everyone's help, I got through the play without any obvious awkward moments which might have been apparent to the audience. Everyone was so kind, and congratulated me at the end of the performance – I was quite numb by then! Obviously we had to rehearse nearly every day that week, and gradually I began to know what I was doing, and to become word perfect. Joan Greenwood was indisposed for the next fortnight; I played the whole week at the Theatre Royal, Newcastle, and also at the Yvonne Arnaud, Guildford, by which time I was actually beginning to enjoy myself! One technical problem I found difficult to surmount; I had to slap John Gregson's face at one point, and was too gentle about it. 'Go on,' he said, 'Hit me hard!' We rehearsed this again and again – sometimes he got a great resounding slap, and sometimes he didn't!

Joan returned to the show after Guildford, but I was asked to remain on the tour as her understudy – goodness knows what they were thinking of in the first place, going out on tour without adequate cover. The next venue was a delightful little theatre at Rosehill, near Whitehaven. It was sponsored by Sekers, the silk people, and the interior was beautifully designed by Oliver Messel. We were a stone's throw from the Lake District, and John was concerned that I was without a car. 'You must see some of this marvellous scenery,' he insisted, and took a couple of us out for the day, round some of the lakes, which were absolutely beautiful. We finished up having a cream tea near Buttermere – a carefree day, with no worries, knowing I almost certainly had no performance to do that night. I shall always remember John Gregson for his kindness, help and friendship – (and what an attractive man he was!)

The only other straight play with which I have been concerned is Chekov's *The Seagull* at the Duke of York's. Again, I was just a walking understudy to Madam Arkadina (Sheila Ballantyne), but this time did not have the opportunity of going on. However, I was keen to try my hand at Chekov, and the intensive rehearsal I had in the role was very valuable. There were many well-known names in the cast, notably Alan Bates as Trigorin, Robert Flemyng (Sorin), Richard O'Callaghan (Konstantin), and Georgina Hale (Nina). An unexpected bonus I received on the last night was a kiss from Alan Bates!

Musicals still kept turning up; a new production of *Robert and Elizabeth* was on the cards, to open at the Yvonne Arnaud, in Guildford, do a couple more dates, then go off to Canada for a short east coast tour. This idea appealed a lot, for I loved the show, and my old friend Sandy Faris would be conducting. The production was to be directed by Val May, who was director of the Yvonne Arnaud at that time. I auditioned, and was given the role of Wilson, which I had always wanted to play. The three leading roles were impressively cast; Sally Ann Howes was to play Elizabeth Barrett, Jeremy Brett, Robert Browning, and Michael Denison, Mr Barrett. The production, unlike the original which was a lavish musical, took rather more the form of a musical play. Gone were the big dance numbers and the large chorus; the entire cast numbered fewer than two dozen, but this different conception of the piece was stylish, attractive, and equally valid. I found Sally Ann Howes, with whom I had many scenes, friendly and pleasant to work with. I shared a dressing room with Lucy Fenwick, who was to play

Barrett's niece Bella Hedley, and I don't think my life has ever been the same since.

Robert and Elizabeth received good press in Guildford, and all seemed set for a successful Canadian tour. Everything went smoothly, but I do remember a rather hysterical incident one night, when the set changed from Wimpole Street to Elizabeth's bedroom. The change was effected by means of two small revolves; Elizabeth's couch, on which she was lying, was on one of them, and I stood close beside her. This revolve came round as usual, but the one on the opposite side of the stage, for some reason did not turn, and we were left to do the next scene with a pillar box and street lamp in Elizabeth's room. If she asks me to post a letter to Robert, I shan't have far to go, I thought! It is very easy to get a fit of giggles on such occasions, and we were no exception to the rule!

Another amusing (though not to me) incident occurred during my first entrance. Elizabeth's dog, Flush, (for some reason played by a Cavalier King Charles spaniel, though it should have been a golden cocker spaniel) was exemplary. She jumped on and off the sofa at the slightest command, came when she was called, and generally behaved herself. We had the same little dog for every performance in England, and she was absolutely no trouble at all. But in Canada I had a new Flush in every city, which made life rather difficult. On my first entrance I had to take the dog on stage on a lead and sing, 'Dragged by a spaniel up Wimpole Street, Oxford Street and Cavendish Square' etc. It usually worked fairly well, but in one place I was landed with a very fat Flush who had a will of his own. I got him on stage all right, but he promptly slipped his collar and made a rapid exit, leaving me to sing my solo foolishly dangling a lead with an empty collar on the end of it! Not one of my favourite moments.

Our venue in Toronto was a big mistake. We played the O'Keefe Centre – a great barn of a place, when, as a fairly small production we should have been at the Royal Alexandra, just across the road. It was hard to play intimate scenes across the vast acreage of the orchestra pit, and we felt isolated from the audience on that enormous stage, with our modest but effective scenery. The original West End production would have been more at home there. The press hated us, and went to town. 'Barretts, go home!' was the headline in one of the papers after the first night. Not all the reviews were as unkind as that, and the audiences seemed to enjoy the show, so we just got on with it.

The weather was bitterly cold during our stay in Canada, but there are so many subways and underground shopping malls that it is easy to keep warm. In Ottawa we found we could get from our hotel to the theatre without surfacing once. I shared a hotel room as well as a dressing room with Lucy Fenwick, as we found we got on really well together. Things were never dull. She is a unique person, with a zany sense of humour which appealed to me enormously, and which proved to be very refreshing on a long tour. The company were a gregarious lot, and always arranging meals or parties after the show, to which everyone was invited. This was all very well, but eight shows a week are quite hard going, and Lucy and I preferred to go back to the hotel most nights for a quiet glass of wine and a bit of relaxation. Besides, no matter how much you enjoy the company of your fellow

artists, you don't necessarily want to spend all your free time
with them. We got rather bored with the constant 'We're
going to a marvellous restaurant tonight, then on to a club –
oh, do come – you must!' 'I'm getting tired of this,' said Lucy.
'What can we do?' Then an idea came to us. One night,
after the show, we dressed up in our most glamorous clothes,
did our hair, put on lots of jewellery, and went to the stage
door, where everyone was gathering for that night's
entertainment. 'Wherever are you going?' they asked in
amazement, eyeing us suspiciously, thinking we were off to
meet a couple of handsome hunks – (if only!) 'Oh, just out,'
we answered airily, 'Taxi!' And we sallied forth in all our
finery – straight back to our hotel, where we were in bed,
shrieking with laughter half an hour later! That did the trick,
everyone thought we were otherwise engaged, and we were
left in peace, only going out after the show when we felt like
it.

The Theatre Royal, Plymouth, has many happy memories
for me, both as a performer and a director. Stephen
Sondheim's *Sweeney Todd*, and *The Music Man*, (Meredith
Wilson), both directed by David Kelsey, provided me with
two very rewarding roles. The former is another of my
favourite musicals – really more of an opera. I had wanted
to play Mrs Lovett, but the role had already been cast, so I
was offered the Beggar Woman. She is a sad, pathetic
creature, who has been subjected to such horrors that she
has become deranged – a wonderful and challenging part to
play, and one I very much enjoyed. It's a revolting and
macabre tale, and Sondheim wrote music to match the mood
– difficult music, too – you must be on your toes all the time
in order not to miss an entrance or fail to pitch an unlikely

note. We played in the Drum, at the Theatre Royal – an intimate studio theatre with versatile facilities that can include a thrust stage, as used for this production. The set was remarkable, with an upstairs which housed the dreaded barber's chair – the original one from the Drury Lane production. When we saw it first, we regarded it doubtfully. 'I'm not going down in that,' said Ray Marlowe, who was playing the Judge – one of the characters to suffer Sweeney's razor – 'I've got trouble with my back as it is.' Hearing this, some of the others looked decidedly dubious. I foresaw problems and thought it time to act. 'Oh, there's nothing to it,' I declared, leaping into the chair. 'Pull the lever, boys!' This was done, the chair tipped forwards, and I shot down the chute to the floor below, landing on the mattress placed there for that purpose. Jane Egan (Joanna) sized up the situation at once. 'My turn next!' she shouted, taking her place in the chair and sliding down the chute with a theatrical shriek. The flood gates were opened – everyone (except Ray) was queueing up for a ride, whether they had to use the chair in the performance or not. We intrepid females had led the way – the men could hardly stand back and look like cowards! Eventually Ray tried out the chair, with much persuasion, and many groans as he arrived at the bottom – he continued to moan and complain every night as he slid down the chute to join me on the mattress! I can't say I ever really enjoyed it – the moment before the lever was pulled and the trap opened in front of you was always a bit tense, but the contraption was tested before each show, so we took it on trust.

The cast of *Sweeney* was a strong one; Michael Maurel, a fine operatic baritone was formidable in the title role, and

Eileen Gourlay an excellent Mrs Lovett – in fact, I could not fault any performance. I must mention especially Jane's characterisation of Joanna – just the right mix of sweetness and vulnerability, and beautifully sung. But there was one exceptionally fine portrayal of the Italian barber, Pirelli, whose impeccable diction and splendid voice proclaimed his origins – he was none other than Gareth Jones – another ex-D'Oyly Carte performer. I seemed to be meeting them in all sorts of shows, and they invariably had that unique aura of quality.

The Drum seemed a far cry from the Theatre Royal, Drury Lane, where I had first seen *Sweeney Todd* and been so impressed with it, but I felt that the intimate, almost claustrophobic atmosphere of the smaller theatre, together with the proximity of the audience, magnified the brooding evil of mid-nineteenth century London. As a note in the programme read: 'Tonight you will be closer to the razor's edge than ever before...'

I had the pleasure of working at Plymouth again with David Kelsey, this time in *The Music Man*, which was staged in the main theatre. I played the Irish mother of the heroine, Mrs Paroo, which gave me great scope for a fairly improbable brogue! The show was fun to do; Martin Waddington, who had shown such skill with Sweeney Todd, was the musical director, and the cast were extremely talented. And who was the Music Man himself? None other than Leon Greene – yet another ex-D'Oyly Carte performer. I couldn't seem to get away from them!

I spent a very pleasant season at Chichester one summer in a musical version of Peter Ustinov's *Romanov and Juliet*. Wendy Toye was the director, and Sandy Faris had written the music, which I thought delightful; it was tuneful, inventive, and original. The fact that the show failed to attract much interest was in no way due to the score – or the lyrics (by Julian More) which were both witty and very funny. Somehow the whole thing just didn't seem to work. I believe the management had tried to persuade Peter Ustinov to play the General – his original role in the play – but he declined, perhaps because he was no singer. But even so, I believe he would have been far superior to Topol, who I suppose was expected to be a crowd-puller. He didn't seem to have much interest in the show, and I was not at all impressed with his performance, which seemed perfunctory and quite disinterested.

I was involved in a not very happy twelve week season at the Palace Court Theatre, Bournemouth one summer in *Lock up your Daughters*, a bawdy musical restoration comedy which had originally been presented at the Mermaid Theatre. I played Mrs Squeezum, with a very well-known television actor as my opposite number, Justice Squeezum. He did not like anyone other than himself to get a laugh, and would do his best to see that they did not. I had a marvellous exit line at one point, which got a round of applause and a big laugh on the first night, but on the second, absolute silence. What had gone wrong, I wondered, until I was told by someone who was watching the scene that my 'husband', not liking my laugh at all, went to the far corner of the stage and did a comic piece of business as soon as my back was turned. This of course caused the eyes of the audience to switch immediately to him, while I slipped off the stage unnoticed. He was an objectionable man in all respects, and the fact that he took to coming into my dressing room every night wearing nothing but a bowler hat (not a pretty sight) did nothing to impress me otherwise. I took to hiding behind a rack of costumes in the men's dressing room till he had gone. 'Where's Cynthia?' I would hear him say, but the boys never gave me away! I saw him quite recently playing a dear old man in a television series. If only the viewers knew the truth, I thought! He was replaced by Brendan Barry, a very fine actor, after a few weeks, I'm glad to say. Rumour reached us that his characterisation of Justice Squeezum, together with the obscene gestures he used on stage, were unsuitable for the Bournemouth audiences! Life – and the show – certainly looked up after his departure.

There's only one more musical that I feel deserves a mention; I remember it with great affection, though it was terribly hard work. The production was staged at the Sherman Theatre, Cardiff, and the show was *Something's Afoot* – described as 'a murder mystery musical'. It was actually a very funny send-up of an Agatha Christie-style story, with absolutely everyone getting murdered in all kinds of improbable ways by the end of the show. We had three and a half weeks rehearsal time, then two and a half weeks of performances. That doesn't sound too bad, but I as Miss Tweed (an obvious caricature of Miss Marple) was not murdered till almost the end of the show, and had a daunting amount of dialogue – musical numbers as well. I recorded it all on tape, and used to go to bed with my headphones on, listening till the small hours in the hope that it would all go in somehow. It did, of course, just in time for the opening night, but I could not let my concentration slip for one moment during the show or I would be in trouble. The character of Miss Tweed was quite unlike anything else I had done, so it was a challenge, and one which I believe I coped with successfully. I was pleased with the press comments next day, one of which I quote: 'Although all members of the cast contribute significantly, the performance of Cynthia Morey as the elderly amateur detective Miss Tweed really shines through, forming the hub around which *Something's Afoot* revolves'. (Western Mail). Perhaps it's not very modest of me to quote that, but learning the show in time was such a mammoth task, and what a relief it was to know that all the hard work had paid off.

There are so many more things I could have included in this chapter – appearing at the National in *Night of a Thousand Stars*, taking part in an excerpt from *Me and My Girl*, at the Laurence Olivier Awards, and being part of the *Anything Goes* team at the Queen Mother's 90th Birthday Tribute at the Palladium. But it's time to go back to Gilbert and Sullivan, where my theatrical career began, and who seem to pursue me down the years! One thing I must mention before we leave the mighty world of musicals – after the Queen Mother's show, we were waiting around at the stage door of the Palladium for transport back to the Prince Edward, and I noticed Sir John Gielgud sitting by himself outside. He had done a most wonderful reading, and I thought I must tell him how moved I had been. He clutched my hand, and said, 'Oh, darling – I was *so* nervous!' I was touched by his humility – an example to all of us.

12.

So here we are – full circle. I began my career all those years ago – 1951 – in Gilbert and Sullivan, and finished with those two gentlemen, or so I thought, in 1957. More than forty years later I find myself once more involved! Mind you, they've kept popping up now and then to remind me of their existence – I've decided not to fight them any more – I know when I'm beaten!

Trial by Jury seems to have a way of intruding on my life in various shapes and forms. In the late seventies Leonard Osborn and I were asked to produce a concert for the Bar Musical Society in Middle Temple Hall, the first half of which was *Trial*. The second half was to have been *Cox and Box*, but owing to illness (I can't remember whose) we had to substitute 'A G&S Miscellany'. This worked out wonderfully well, and the highlight of the evening was John Reed singing 'When I went to the Bar' (*Iolanthe*) as a duet with the 'real' Lord Chancellor, Lord Hailsham! That caused quite a sensation! I browsed through the programme just before writing this, to find all sorts of familiar names taking part. The cast of *Trial* was: Judge: John Reed; Defendant: Geoffrey Shovelton; Usher: John Broad; Counsel: Michael Tuckey, and Plaintiff: Barbara Lilley. Some of those names are as familiar today as they were then, but I wonder what happened to the others? It would be interesting to know – maybe they'll turn up at Buxton one day! Royston Nash conducted, and the entertainment took place in the gracious presence of the Queen Mother.

The next *Trial* that springs to mind was at the Mansion House. The Lord Mayor of that year (1987), Sir David Rowe-Hamm, had announced that he wished to play the Learned Judge at a charity evening in aid of the Prince's Youth Business Trust. I was asked to stage the show, which was to be the cabaret before a champagne reception and buffet supper, with David Mackie to conduct. Several rehearsals were necessary to coach Sir David in his role of the Judge (he had played it at school) – and the hospitality David and I received at the Mansion House before, during and after these sessions was formidable. They were always in the afternoons, and the dainty tea which preceded them was fine; but out came the gin and tonic in due course, and rehearsal became progressively more relaxed! Sir David was really quite good in the part, and absolutely fine on the night. He insisted on being billed as 'Richard Whittington' so that he would remain incognito to all his guests until the last moment, though I'm sure most of his astute friends must have put two and two together! Others in the cast on that occasion were: Geoffrey Shovelton as theDefendant; John Ayldon, Usher; Michael Wakeham, Counsel, and Patricia Cope, Plaintiff. It was a most enjoyable event – so was the supper afterwards.

Another *Trial by Jury* was presented on March 29th 2000 at the Savoy Hotel, marking – almost – the 125th anniversary of the opera. Again I was asked to direct the show, and David Mackie to conduct. It provided the cabaret following a gala dinner, the whole event being in aid of Sargent Cancer Care for Children. The actual day of the performance, fraught though it was, with only the morning to get the whole thing together before a dress rehearsal with orchestra late afternoon, was a thoroughly satisfying experience. David Mackie, who was conducting, got through the tightly-packed schedule with his usual calm efficiency, achieving a wonderful balance between stage and orchestra under really difficult conditions; we had to extend the small cabaret stage in order to accommodate the set, and the orchestra of nineteen players was placed to one side. There were quite a number of problems to solve, but with a cast of pro's, the trauma was minimised, and the busy day of the show was fine. What I really disliked were the months of interminable meetings, the endless discussions, the administrative labyrinths – what on earth, I thought, has all this got to do with *me?* My job is to get the show on, on the night.

Thank heaven for Ken Robertson, who stepped in to stage manage – I don't know what we'd have done without him, or Alan Spencer, whose assistance with the tricky bits of business which help to make *Trial* what it is, was invaluable on such an action-packed day. The orchestra was of an extremely high standard, with many leading London players, producing a quality of sound rarely heard on such occasions. The cast, also, was excellent. We were fortunate to have Marilyn Hill Smith as the Plaintiff – she was charming. Gareth Jones played the Judge, John Ayldon the Usher; Stephen Brown, the Defendant (now, there's a young tenor worth watching). And John Fryatt made his debut as the Counsel, playing it so well that everyone thought he'd done it hundreds of times. Between the dress rehearsal and the performance there was a very long wait, but everyone, cast, orchestra and all concerned, were given supper in the Parlour – an enormous room to the rear of the Lancaster Room, where the function took place. It was good to see old colleagues sitting round catching up on news and gossip, and a pleasant atmosphere built up for the show – much less formal and more congenial than in the Lancaster Room, where I joined some of the patrons for the performance!

Yet another *Trial* was to come, the following June. Melvyn Tarran, well-known in Gilbert and Sullivan circles for his Oak Hall Manor concerts and his remarkable collection of G&S memorabilia, decided to put on a Gala 2000 concert at the Hawth Theatre, Crawley, and asked me to help. I thought hard about it; we wanted to do *Trial*, but had there been too many productions recently, we wondered? We must try to make it a concert with a difference. David Steadman had been asked to conduct; he had written a new overture featuring excerpts from all the Savoy operas neatly and cleverly woven together – that would make a wonderful opening. I then had the idea to follow this with a short playlet telling how *Trial* had come into being; this featured Gilbert, Sullivan and Richard D'Oyly Carte, and lasted only about five or six minutes. It was performed in front of a gauze, behind which the cast of *Trial by Jury* were assembled, ready to begin. On Sullivan's agreeing to set Gilbert's libretto to music, the two men shook hands, which was the cue for the opening music to begin. The light began to bleed slowly through the gauze on to the set where the cast were 'frozen' in a picture which gradually came to life, and the show started. This worked well, but oh, for more rehearsal time to work on detail and effect. I was again grateful to Alan Spencer for helping so much with the chorus moves, leaving me free to attend to other things. David Mackie conducted *Trial*, so there was nothing to worry about from the musical angle. The orchestra was composed mainly of the players who had done the Savoy event, and again we had an excellent quality of sound. The three men in the playlet – Charles Pemberton giving his splendid portrayal of W S Gilbert, Anthony Herrick (my very own cousin!) looking remarkably like Sullivan, and the well-known actor Michael Simkins as D'Oyly Carte, made the most of their brief appearances. G & S enthusiasts who were unable to attend the concert (the eight hundred-seater theatre was sold out, and some unfortunate people were turned away) will no doubt be interested to hear who was singing in *Trial*. Gareth Jones was to have played the Judge, but at rather short notice was unable to do so. David Steadman had the idea of asking Donald Francke, who had played the role in the Bow Street *Trial*, if he'd be willing to step in. Donald agreed – luckily for us; he was currently in *The Phantom of the Opera*, and kindly came down to the Hawth on the Sunday morning, after two performances the previous day. Joseph Shovelton, of the New D'Oyly Carte, played the Defendant; John Broad, the Usher; Kenneth Sandford, Counsel; and Jill Washington, the Plaintiff. Bruce Graham was the Foreman of the Jury, which was filled with former D'Oyly Carte members, as was the public box. We had eight bridesmaids, (as, I believe, did the original 1875 production), five of whom were young but experienced G&S performers; the other three might have been a tiny bit more mature, but they looked just as youthful under the lights! It is really good to see young singers doing so well on the Gilbert and Sullivan scene, and we managed to have a fair number of fresh faces on stage among our older performers.

That was only the first half of the concert. We wanted the second half to consist of numbers from all the Savoy operas, in chronological order, but how to present them in a novel way? I decided to have two compères – one good, the other evil, who would appear from either side of the stage between numbers to comment on the next opera and the current situation between Gilbert, Sullivan and D'Oyly Carte. For ease of learning the script, which was in rhyming couplets, and getting together to rehearse, John Fryatt played the evil one (Demon Discord) and I, the good (Fairy Concord). The dialogue was sometimes quite caustic; there was no love lost between us! Plenty of good things abounded (so many successes) for me to boast of, but also bad ones (the frequent disagreements, the carpet quarrel) for the Demon Discord to gloat over, but of course, good triumphs in the end, as always. Our costumes were beautifully designed and made for us by John King, who had worked at the Royal Opera House and at Glyndebourne. With great co-operation from David Steadman in the pit, the whole thing seemed to go with a bang, and I really do think the new approach made a difference. It was fun writing the script, and of course John made his usual invaluable contribution. Dare I quote one of his lines – here goes!

> Fairy C: That Demon Discord pains me sorely –
> Demon D: I love being creepy here in Crawley!

It goes without saying that poetic gem got the most enormous laugh!

We had a very good line-up of soloists for the second half, and it is hard to single out any in particular. I must say, however, that I have never heard 'Minerva', sung by Yvonne Patrick, more beautifully performed. Another memorable item was 'Alone, and Yet Alive' poignantly sung by Helen

Landis, looking exquisite in a gorgeous cream creation. Stephen Davis is a young baritone who obviously has a rosy future – but it's unfair to pick out a few artists when the general standard was so high. And of course Tom Round was there – he only had to show his face to attract ecstatic applause – but when he started to do the hornpipe after Dick Dauntless's song, the delight of the audience knew no bounds. Melvyn was hoping the Gala 2000 might be a success, but I think he was overwhelmed by the response it received. I'm glad of that, for he put so much effort into getting it all together. Not only had he assembled many D'Oyly Carte artists on stage, there were also a number of celebrity guests in the audience. Among them was Helen Roberts, a well-known principal soprano who had joined the company in 1938! Another favourite of much more recent years was Valerie Masterson, who has gone on to receive such acclaim in grand opera, but who, like so many of us has retained her love for Gilbert and Sullivan.

I was asked to devise a G & S cabaret for the Grosvenor House Hotel, and wondered what might be possible without resorting to a string of songs or excerpts from the operas. I finally wrote a potted version of *HMS Pinafore*, with Buttercup telling the story. Some of the numbers had to be abridged, and big choruses cut, but it lent itself surprisingly well to this treatment, and the audience got a comprehensive, if condensed version. It must have worked successfully, as we were subsequently asked to perform it at the Hilton and the Inn on the Park. I found the programmes the other day; John Reed played Sir Joseph on one occasion, John Fryatt took over for the next; Philip Potter or Geoffrey Shovelton sang Ralph, Jennifer Toye, Josephine, Tom Lawlor, Captain

Corcoran, and either I or Eileen Shaw played Buttercup.
The audiences, which always included many Americans,
seemed to appreciate the shows thoroughly. Albert Truelove,
as usual, was a great help in borrowing D'Oyly Carte
costumes and arranging props.

Some interesting work came my way via the Plymouth-based
television company Westward TV in the shape of an amusing
documentary entitled *The Pirates of the Pirates of Penzance*.
This set out to re-create in an amusing way the first
impromptu performance of *Pirates* at the tiny Bijou Theatre,
Paignton, on December 30th 1879. At the same time a
performance would be given in New York, thus establishing
the copyright and preventing the 'pirating' of the opera –
hence the title of the film. My job was to direct the *Pirates*
excerpts, though I ended up also appearing in the film as
Ruth, played on that occasion by Fanny Harrison. I insisted
that John Reed should come to play the Major General; Ian
Wallace was the Sergeant of the Police, and Spike Milligan,
a rather eccentric commentator on the whole improbable
affair!

The Bijou Theatre had long since been engulfed by the
Gerston Hotel and adjacent shops, so the venue chosen for
filming this bizarre premiere of *Pirates* was a small Victorian
church hall, which, with a few embellishments looked
remarkably like a little theatre of that time. Backstage was
unbelievably primitive, with battered old oil stoves
inefficiently heating what passed for dressing rooms. I
cherish a memory of Ian Wallace, John and myself crouching
over one of these, exchanging stories – and what a raconteur
Ian was – we nearly missed our entrance, listening to his

tales! My part in the film was a shot of Fanny Harrison rehearsing the role of Ruth, in ordinary day clothes; my costume arrived – a smart late Victorian gown in turquoise blue, with a matching hat. It fitted me like a dream, and somehow it seemed very familiar. I looked inside to see if there was a label, and sure enough, there it was: Cynthia Morey. No wonder it fitted so well – it was one of my own costumes from *Gone With the Wind*! We were invited to see a preview of the film later in London, and I thought it worked rather well. It was a novel way to deal with the subject, very amusing, and in its way, quite informative. Transmission took place on a prime viewing date – Boxing Day, 1980.

I must not leave the world of Gilbert and Sullivan without touching upon the subject of amateur societies, for I have directed quite a number of productions, some of which I have enjoyed, and some which I have not. There is one big problem facing directors in this particular field, and that is the lack of commitment from some society members, resulting in a great deal of absence from rehearsals. It is disconcerting to attempt to stage a big number or a dialogue scene with half the cast missing. When they eventually turn up, they do not know what they are doing, the whole thing has to be done again, and no progress is made. I can't imagine why such people think that they need less rehearsal than professionals in order to give a good show. I know that *we* are paid for what we do – it is our job – but amateurs must always remember that audiences are paying to see their show in just the same way, and must always be given the very best possible performance. I realise that domestic emergencies do occasionally prevent people attending rehearsals, but these are relatively rare. One thing is sure – the most talented and able performers always seem to manage to be there. End of lecture!

I have met many singers in amateur societies who, if they had wished, could have been professional performers, and it has been a great pleasure to work with them. It is also very rewarding to work on someone who you believe has great potential, and help them to realise it. I was directing *The Mikado* once, and auditioning several girls for the role of Yum-Yum. There were some very good singers; one girl did not sing quite as well as the others, and seemed rather shy, but she had something indefinable which made her different from the rest, and which I thought could be worked on. When I told the committee of my choice, they were surprised. 'But so-and-so *always* takes the lead,' they insisted. I gave 'so-and-so' the role of Pitti-Sing – in which she was excellent – but so was my Yum-Yum. She had that quality I was looking for, and only needed confidence and some individual coaching to help her develop the talent I suspected was there. And as she relaxed, her voice improved beyond my expectations, and her singing of The Sun Whose Rays was delightful. 'We'd no idea she could do it!' said the committee.

When I audition potential principals I much prefer them just to walk in and sing the set number in a simple way, using their voice to convey the character they are portraying. I must admit I am rather put off when a would-be Mikado goes into his song with all the moves, gestures and wild laughs that were traditional in the D'Oyly Carte for so many years. Because Donald Adams or John Ayldon always did them, it doesn't follow that they are right for every performer of that role – besides, I may want *my* Mikado to do something entirely different. If I am confronted by a carbon copy, I might possibly have doubts about the candidate's ability to adapt to any changes I have in mind.

I admire tradition; I also like new ideas. The two things are not necessarily incompatible. I directed two productions some years ago for the Plymouth Gilbert and Sullivan Fellowship at the Theatre Royal. One was *Iolanthe*. The year was 1983; the announcement of the date of a general election was imminent. I wonder if Gilbert would have taken that into account? At all events, I did. My Fairy Queen just had to be modelled on Margaret Thatcher; luckily the talented contralto who played her was able to achieve exactly that unmistakable quality of voice for the dialogue. The audience loved it, and when she got to 'Let me see – I've a borough or two at my disposal – How would you like to go into parliament?' the house went mad. That, apart from the blue rosette worn by the Fairy Queen, was the only innovation we made. I believe something similar was done in the *Ratepayers' Iolanthe*, but that was much later. The society was honoured to have John Reed himself to play the Lord Chancellor, so a great success and record audiences were guaranteed.

The second opera I directed for Plymouth was *Pirates*, and I decided on a rather different approach for this. I know there has been a lot of tiresome updating of operas and plays in recent years, but in 1984 such a practice was comparatively new. I pondered over the libretto, and when I reached the girls' dialogue after their opening chorus in Act I, and read 'And I wonder where Papa is? We have left him ever so far behind' and the bit about mermaids – 'Tails they may, but feet they cannot!' it struck me that these girls sounded awfully like 'flappers' – why not set *Pirates* in the 1920s? 'Ah!' I hear you saying, 'But what about Frederic's 21st birthday in 1940?' Yes, that *was* a problem. I had to resolve this by changing his line to: 'That birthday will not be reached by me till the nineteen-eighties' – I could not be more exact, or it would not have fitted the music. No other word of dialogue was touched, and everything was played absolutely straight. There was one musical innovation: as the girls reached the end of their chorus, the orchestra slipped slickly into the Charleston, and there were sixteen bars – no more – of dancing. The applause at the end of this was deafening, and there certainly could have been at least one encore, but we decided that some of the magic would be lost if we repeated it. The wisdom of this decision was endorsed by one of the critics next day: 'Miss Morey has given the opera some updating, but her fresh touches are colouring only on the original, and nothing is done to excess – such moments as the Charleston dancing are never overplayed.' Just what I had intended.

One more important point about the Plymouth *Pirates*; I had set it round about 1927, and was lucky enough to find an Austin 7 of exactly that date – so what could be better than the arrival of the Major General in that vehicle, complete with chauffeur? Especially as the role was played by John Fryatt, who made the most of the situation. I insisted that the little car took part in the curtain call – after all, it was one of the stars of the show.

Way back in 1979 I had the idea that a Victorian pantomime could be devised from the material of the operas, using

Gilbert's characters and Sullivan's music. After much consideration I decided that the subject most suitable for this project was *The Sleeping Beauty*. There were a lot of parallel situations: what better than Phoebe's song at the spinning wheel for the wicked fairy, about to prick the Princess's finger with the lethal spindle? And the scene in *The Sorcerer*, when the villagers fall asleep under the spell of the love potion would be perfect for the similar scene in the pantomime when the Princess and the court succumb to the hundred years' sleep. So, in collaboration with John Fryatt, after many meetings and regular frenzied phone calls, we eventually finished the script and compiled the score. This all happened over a number of years, as we were both very busy. I was approached by the Sale Gilbert and Sullivan Society, who wanted put it on in January, 1987. I would have directed it myself, but had just been invited to play the Wicked Fairy in the Players' pantomime, so Roberta Morrell kindly stepped in and took over, with Alistair Donkin playing Mad Meg, the Wicked Witch. The weather was appalling during performance week, with heavy snow making roads treacherous and people reluctant to go out. Audiences were consequently thin, and while I understand that it met with general approval, it didn't really have a fair trial.

In 1991 I received a phone call from Jean Bruce, of the Oast Theatre, Tonbridge. 'I believe you have a Gilbert and Sullivan pantomime,' she said, 'We'd be interested to put it on.' So *The Sleeping Beauty of Savoy* received its southern premiere – and a delightful one, too. The Oast is a wonderful little theatre, and our show was presented in a charming and witty way, beautifully dressed (by the Oast Theatre Wardrobe) and directed by Jean. It ran for ten days, was sold out, and I have never really understood why more societies don't put it on. But then, of course, I'm prejudiced!

Oak Hall Manor in the lovely Sussex countryside is the venue for many intimate concerts organised by Melvyn Tarran, a large number of which are Gilbert and Sullivan orientated. I have been involved in several of these; they seem to start as small affairs, but often tickets are sold in such numbers that Melvyn is obliged to have a marquee erected in the courtyard where a delicious supper is served afterwards. One enjoyable event was a tribute to Isabel Jay, one of the very early D'Oyly Carte principal sopranos who went on to star in many West End musical comedies. There was much research to do, old out-of-print scores to find, and recordings to locate. I wrote and compèred the concert, which was preceded by a slide show of Isabel Jay photographs, presented by John Cannon. The event was made even more interesting by the presence of Isabel's daughter – a very attractive lady in her nineties. Other Oak Hall entertainments with which I have been involved were a tribute to Peter Pratt and Leonard Osborn, both of whom I worked with in the fifties, and a 'Three Tenors' concert. In this, three of our bright young tenors of today, Stephen Brown, David Menezes and Mark Guerin masqueraded as three famous D'Oyly Carte tenors – Courtice Pounds, Tom Round and Derek Oldham respectively. Each sang songs from roles played by their heroes, both Gilbert and Sullivan and others. The situation was quite amusing, for Tom was sitting in the audience, having given a talk on his reminiscences that afternoon!

As the years go by, members of the old D'Oyly Carte company are, sadly but inevitably, becoming fewer in number. Many of them are still performing brilliantly, and continuing to delight their audiences. But the time is coming when we must look to young performers to carry into the future these operas we love so much. The International Gilbert and Sullivan Festival does a very good job in this respect at Buxton every summer. It always gives me great pleasure to see young folk taking part in productions with such enthusiasm, and walking round the town in sweat shirts emblazoned with the name of their society and the opera they are performing. We need this commitment and energy if the Gilbert and Sullivan operas are to survive and flourish.

Most importantly, the new D'Oyly Carte Opera Company seems to be going from strength to strength. It has been heart-warming to see that name back at the Savoy. After all – that is where it belongs.

Oh, one more thing –
My first book, *Inclined to Dance and Sing* was on sale at the G&S Festival last year, and as I was leaving the Paxton Suite after taking part in an entertainment, I was accosted by a lady clutching a copy. 'Just bought your book,' she said, 'I wanted something to read in bed, and I've finished my Harry Potter!'

What an act to follow!